# EQUITY AS PRAXIS IN EARLY CHILDHOOD EDUCATION AND CARE

# EQUITY AS PRAXIS IN EARLY CHILDHOOD EDUCATION AND CARE

Edited by
Zuhra Abawi,
Ardavan Eizadirad,
and Rachel Berman

CANADIAN
SCHOLARS

Toronto | Vancouver

**Equity as Praxis in Early Childhood Education and Care**
Edited by Zuhra Abawi, Ardavan Eizadirad, and Rachel Berman

First published in 2021 by
**Canadian Scholars, an imprint of CSP Books Inc.**
425 Adelaide Street West, Suite 200
Toronto, Ontario
M5V 3C1

**www.canadianscholars.ca**

**Library and Archives Canada Cataloguing in Publication**

Title: Equity as praxis in early childhood education and care / edited by Zuhra Abawi,
    Ardavan Eizadirad, and Rachel Berman.
Names: Abawi, Zuhra E., editor. | Eizadirad, Ardavan, editor. | Berman, Rachel, 1965- editor.
Description: Includes bibliographical references.
Identifiers: Canadiana (print) 20210162252 | Canadiana (ebook) 2021016249X |
    ISBN 9781773382616 (softcover) | ISBN 9781773382623 (PDF) |
    ISBN 9781773382630 (EPUB)
Subjects: LCSH: Early childhood education—Social aspects—Ontario. | LCSH: Child
    care—Social aspects—Ontario. | LCSH: Children of minorities—Education (Early
    childhood)—Ontario. | LCSH: Children of minorities—Care—Ontario. |
    LCSH: Critical pedagogy—Ontario. | LCSH: Culturally relevant pedagogy—Ontario. |
    LCSH: Educational equalization—Ontario.
Classification: LCC LB1139.3.C3 E78 2021 | DDC 372.2109713—dc23

Cover design by Rafael Chimicatti
Cover image © Strekalova | Dreamstime.com
Page layout by S4Carlisle Publishing Services


21  22  23  24  25        5  4  3  2  1

Printed and bound in Ontario, Canada

I dedicate this book to my aunties, Zuhra and Jinia, who died during childhood in Afghanistan. Your memory will always live on in my heart.

*Zuhra Abawi*

I dedicate this body of work to my partner, Ciara John, my community of Scarborough, my home country of Iran, and to everyone around the world who fights unjust systems and their inequitable laws, policies, and practices. Love and hope will always overcome fear and hopelessness. In the face of injustice, we will flourish by uniting, mobilizing, adapting, and growing collectively.

*Ardavan Eizadirad*

I dedicate this book to early childhood educators: early childhood educators who are working in a fragmented and difficult system with ever more surveillance and lack of support; early childhood educators who have experienced how exclusionary theories lead to exclusionary practices; and early childhood educators who are working to open their hearts and minds as they are challenged to think, practise, and advocate in new ways so that all children and families, and all early childhood educators, may belong.

*Rachel Berman*

# CONTENTS

Foreword    ix
*Judith K. Bernhard*

Introduction: Healing and Hoping in Community and Love as a Tool for
Advancing Equity as Praxis    xiii
*Zuhra Abawi, Ardavan Eizadirad, and Rachel Berman*

Chapter 1    State of Emergency: Mapping Inequities in Early
Childhood Education and Care in Canada    1
*Ardavan Eizadirad and Zuhra Abawi*

Chapter 2    Low-Income Racialized Children and Access to Quality
ECEC in Ontario    21
*Alana Butler*

Chapter 3    Troubling Dominant Discourses and Stories that Shape
Our Understanding of the Child Refugee    43
*Nidhi Menon*

Chapter 4    Equity Enacted: Possibilities for Difference in ECEC
through a Critical Ethics of Care Approach    65
*Alana Powell, Lisa Johnston, and Rachel Langford*

Chapter 5    Planning Time for Equity: A (Re)Examination of a Study
of ECEs' Perspectives on Planning Time in Southern
Ontario    85
*Lisa Johnston*

Chapter 6    Using Femme Theory to Foster a Feminine-Inclusive Early
Childhood Education and Care Practice    107
*Adam Davies and Rhea Ashley Hoskin*

Chapter 7    Making Space for Indigenous Knowledge in an Urban
             Child-Care Centre    125
             *Maya-Rose Simon*

Chapter 8    Failure and Loss as a Methodological, Relational, and
             Ethical Necessity in Teaching and Learning in the Early
             Years    147
             *Maria Karmiris*

Chapter 9    Reflect, Enact, and Transform: A Preliminary Anti-Racism
             Guide for Early Childhood Educators    165
             *Kerry-Ann Escayg*

**Conclusion: Some Concluding Thoughts on Equity as Praxis**    181
*Rachel Berman*

**Contributor Biographies**    183

# FOREWORD

*Judith K. Bernhard*

The field of Canadian early childhood education (ECE) has relied on multicultural policies that, although well-intentioned, do not seem to have much effect when it comes to reducing the negative outcomes of children growing up in newcomer, Indigenous, and racialized families. Some members of the profession have been reluctant to accept evidence of systemic biases in the system.

As a Latina, my work with Latin American families has brought to light crucial features of the ECE system, in Canada and elsewhere. For example, having investigated some of the causes of Latinx children's low performance—as officially measured—in the school system, I found that many parents are not aware of the systems that determine their children's classroom placement. The result is that children often develop disadvantages of which their parents are barely aware. Without their knowing, these children tend to be overrepresented in some special-needs programs and under-represented in those aimed at so-called gifted students. Present-day report cards, intentionally worded to convey positivity, obscure these dynamics. Parents, moreover, do not know there is an established process for arriving at certain diagnoses, or that there might be some long-term consequences of their child's placement. What each parent wants is to make sure their children succeed in school. But without understanding how the system works, they face many perils along the way.

The negative outcomes of racism are well-known, and yet most teachers deny that there are instances of racism in child-care centres. In fact, children as young as six months can identify skin colour, and by three years of age they are able to state a clear skin-colour preference. Indeed, children are very aware of race from an early age; they enforce groupings and decide who plays with whom according to skin colour, even if teachers are often unaware of this fact. The remedies to systemic racism and bias, then, are neither simple nor obvious. The issues undergirding teachers' blindness is not "fixed" simply by making them aware of the problem, though that would be a first step. Systemic bias must be dealt with at various levels in the educational system. The contributors to this volume are to be commended for clearly articulating anti-racist and anti-bias strategies.

Systemic disadvantages show up in many other ways as well. In many child-care settings, there is not a single person in charge who speaks the language of a majority of the children; in the rare case there is such linguistic representation, it is in the form of an assistant or a cleaner who represents a certain cultural group. Often, the parents of these children are therefore encouraged to abandon use of their first language at home as soon as possible. How can these children grow up to be proud of their families, languages, identities, and communities? It is not, then, simply a matter of helping teachers develop "cultural sensitivity," though that is one step.

More broadly, all children continue to be categorized and evaluated with tools that purport to be universal. These are claimed to be gender-neutral, race-neutral, class-neutral, and so on. It is a feature of the system, therefore, that these children are labelled as deficient based on ostensibly universal norms. The outcome of these practices is poor achievement against several key milestones, including the grade 4 slump, the EQAO (Education Quality and Accountability Office) reading tests, and IQ scores. Paulo Freire, a Brazilian educator, dealt with some of these issues in his well-known book *Pedagogy of the Oppressed* (1970), and his legacy is carried on by the contributors to this volume. Parents of all backgrounds need to become informed and involved when it comes to their children's education. But how do educators help them overcome the barriers currently in place? This problem is addressed in the following chapters.

In the struggle to change the educational system and resulting outcomes for minorities or groups that face systemic bias, the concept of equity has become crucial. Giving children *equal* access to "universal" measures is not a solution since the result is unjust and inequitable outcomes. *Equality* of opportunity is not sufficient, either. The pursuit of equitable outcomes aims at a broader goal. It means that all children, whether Latino, Black, Indigenous, LGBTQ, or from other backgrounds, will fully develop as proud, functioning individuals in their communities. Representatives of these groups should be present at all levels of the education system, including the relevant government ministries. The authors of this book explore ways in which early childhood professionals can contest the system and be part of the broader fight, at all levels, for equitable representation and practices.

As Zuhra Abawi, Ardavan Eizadirad, and Rachel Berman point out in their introduction to this collection, it is time to stir the very foundations of the field of early childhood studies. This volume goes a long way toward contesting enduring inequities in the field.

# Healing and Hoping in Community and Love as a Tool for Advancing Equity as Praxis

*Zuhra Abawi, Ardavan Eizadirad, and Rachel Berman*

Freire (1970) in *Pedagogy of the Oppressed* defines praxis as "reflection and action upon the world" (p. 51) by which, via dialogue, critical consciousness, and a problem-posing model of education, one can begin to critically analyze power dynamics in order to incite change. By interrogating power dynamics involved in the normalization and perpetuation of oppression, and by capitalizing on one's capacity to make a change, we can, as individuals and institutions, challenge inequitable practices for transformative change and liberation. Equity as praxis is about taking a moment to reflect, hope, and heal in community, and to envision alternatives and new beginnings.

Equity as praxis is also about critically analyzing ideologies that have been normalized in the field of early childhood education and care (ECEC) and that currently disadvantage many identities and communities across Canada, particularly Black, Indigenous, and people of colour (BIPOC), those from a lower socio-economic status, the disability community, and Two-Spirit, lesbian, gay, bisexual, pansexual, transgender, gender independent, queer, and questioning (2SLGBTQ+)

communities (Abawi & Berman, 2019; Butler et al., 2019; Colour of Poverty, n.d.; Eizadirad, 2019; United Way Greater Toronto, 2019). As much as this book, and the larger moment in which it is situated, is about reflection and critique, it is just as much about taking action in different forms and mediums and in our various positionalities to advance the field of ECEC and make it more equitable for children, families, early childhood educators, and all other practitioners who work in early year settings. Further, as readers will discover, this text focuses significantly on race in an often colour-blind context of early childhood education, as well as in light of anti-Black racism, Islamophobia, and anti-Indigenous racism permeating settler-colonial societies such as Canada.

Mobilizing and taking action against inequities may involve a range of emotions, including anger, frustration, sadness, and even happiness from winning small victories, but through it all, this process is driven by hope, love, compassion, and solidarity cultivated in safe and brave spaces that allow us to belong to a community. Many early childhood educators (ECEs) enter the field out of love and passion and a desire to work with children and make a difference in their lives as caring adults. Equity as praxis is a reminder that love and compassion is at the heart of equity work and the larger effort to build connections with the children, parents, and communities we work with (Miller, 2018; Reyes, 2019).

This book covers a range of topics in a dialogical problem-posing manner, presenting multiple perspectives from various positionalities related to equity as praxis in ECEC. Collectively, the chapters embody the strength in the face of adversity of early childhood educators, most of whom are overworked and underpaid, and their drive to contest and remedy existing inequities in the field from a critical perspective that reflects the needs of identities and communities that have been historic-ally and currently marginalized.

While we recognize there is a lot of work to be done to further ad-vance the field and to centre equity within it, it is just as important that we pay homage to our ancestors for planting the seeds of care and com-passion in us, as these enable us both to engage with equity work and to accept the challenges and emotional labour necessary to mobilizing and taking a stance against the inequities and injustices embedded in

ECEC. It is also important to recognize the many practitioners, scholars, and community activists who have paved the way, made sacrifices, and won small victories for us, as it is thanks to these efforts that we have arrived at our current juncture. This is no hundred-metre sprint; rather, it is a marathon, and we all need to do our part to ensure we are moving in a direction that centres the voices, experiences, and knowledges of the identities and communities that have historically been marginalized in the field of ECEC (Truth and Reconciliation Commission of Canada, 2015). This depends in part on self-care, healing in community, and mobilizing as a collective so as to continue engaging in equity work for the betterment of the field and those it impacts, whether directly or indirectly.

This book is about facilitating critical dialogue, reflecting and re-imagining, and mobilizing within an educational space that is often neglected and rendered undeserving. It is about naming the problem and seeking to mitigate the root causes of existing inequities such as low wages, poor working conditions, and the feminization of poverty. Often excluded from the realm of "education," child care has become a prominent expense for families, many of whom face limited options and choices due to costs and accessibility issues affiliated with long waiting lists. These outcomes can be traced to larger macro-systemic issues rooted in the lack of a cohesive national child-care strategy in Canada, lack of provincial and territorial funding in the field of child care, and the increased privatization of public goods affiliated with neoliberal ideologies that claim to privilege such concepts as "choice" and "options" (Beach & Ferns, 2015; Eizadirad & Portelli, 2018; Friendly & Prentice, 2009; Richardson et al., 2013).

With such pressing social and political concerns, various other inequities in ECEC are often overlooked. ECEC approaches in Canada and the United States continue to be fraught by psychological-developmentalist approaches to children and childhood, which portray a reductive view of children's understandings, negotiations, and engagements with myriad facets of identity (Brown et al., 2010; Escayg et al., 2017; Friendly & Prabhu, 2010; Husband, 2012). From a deficit framework, those who do not progress along rigidly prescribed, Eurocentric developmental trajectories are pathologized and problematized.

When conceptualizing childhood and early learning, racism, 2SLGBTQ+ issues, poverty, sexism, Indigeneity, colonization, and migration and refugee studies are rarely invoked. However, this does not negate their existence, nor the intersectionalities that govern these various frames, regardless of their subsequent marginalization by white, settler-colonial statehood (Thobani, 2007; Tuck & Yang, 2012). While diversity and multiculturalism are often celebrated as national ideals and part of a larger Canadian metanarrative, and are in turn taken up in many ECEC spaces, such discourses tend to obscure the ways in which racialized, Black, and Indigenous communities encounter severe barriers when it comes to accessing resources such as education, housing, employment, and health care (Colour of Poverty, n.d.; United Way Greater Toronto, 2019).

When discussing racialized people throughout this volume, we refer to people of non-European heritage, regardless of whether they were born in Canada. The Greater Toronto Area, Canada's largest metropolis, has consistently been ranked as the poverty capital of Canada, with income disparities between racialized, Indigenous, and white residents at dismal proportions. According to Statistics Canada (2017), 20.8 percent of racialized families live in poverty, compared to 12.2 percent of white families, while the figure for Indigenous families is more than 80 percent. The effects of racism, genocide, and ongoing settler colonialism continue to bar racialized, Black, and Indigenous communities from accessing the same opportunities afforded to white Canadians (Colour of Poverty, n.d.; James & Turner, 2017; Truth and Reconciliation Commission of Canada, 2015). Among other things, this book asks readers to reflect on how we discuss these issues and to recognize which narratives are normalized—and for what purposes—within mainstream media and which are silenced.

*Equity as Praxis in Early Childhood Education and Care* offers an interdisciplinary, multi-faceted approach to rethinking identities and ways of engaging in praxis in early learning spaces. The ECEC landscape is informed by colour-blindness (Berman et al., 2017; Bonilla-Silva, 2006) and neutrality, a position that perpetuates the notion that children are too young to notice differences among and between people. This notion is simply unfounded, as studies suggest that children as young as two years of age are aware of differences between individuals (Aboud, 1988). Furthermore, an analysis of previous research undertaken by Escayg et al. (2017) lamented that racialized children between the ages of three and five already exhibit pro-white biases.

This textbook seeks to challenge and disrupt developmentalist discourses that frame young children as oblivious, unaware, and incapable of navigating the complexities of multi-faceted identities. Early learning spaces are not neutral sites: they are embedded in power relations informed by racialized, ableist, heteronormative, and gendered hierarchies. The volume provides counter-stories (Berman & Abawi, 2019; Eizadirad, 2019; Ladson-Billings, 1998; Matias, 2013) that seek to upend Eurocentric and developmentalist constructions by drawing on author positionalities, epistemologies, and pedagogies to reconceptualize ECEC in more equitable, counter-normative ways. In this way we hope to contribute to the ongoing dialogue regarding the reframing and rethinking of ECEC assumptions and practices, a movement that has been going on since the late 1980s (for example, see Bloch et al., 2018; Greishaber & Blaise, 2019; Iannacci & Whitty, 2009; Nxumalo & Brown, 2019; Pacini-Ketchabaw & Prochner, 2013).

As much as this textbook offers a critique of the various shortcomings in the field of ECEC, it also embodies the strength and resilience of activists, scholars, and early childhood educators engaged in equity and justice-oriented work in Canada to support children and families in the early years, in some cases in extremely challenging circumstances. A wide range of themes and pedagogies are enclosed in the following chapters, including socialization in childhood, anti-Black racism, neoliberalism, critical feminisms, disability studies, socio-economic status and poverty, refugee and migration studies, and English-language instruction, participatory pedagogy, and the power relations informing equity and inclusive policy enactment. This is not an exhaustive list of the issues we cover in this textbook, but it serves as a starting point from which to engage in important conversations.

Strategically and with intentionality, we have selected a range of authors representing a diversity of experience in the academy as well as the community, from PhD candidates and contract lecturers to new and established professors and practitioners doing various community work with children and families. We feel this perspective from multiple positionalities in the field is required if we are to gain a holistic, interdisciplinary view onto the complexities, contradictions, and nuances in the field of ECEC in Canada.

In chapter 1, Ardavan Eizadirad and Zuhra Abawi explore the discursive changes underlying equity and inclusive education policies pertaining to young children by examining the historical development of ECEC in Canada and its implications for the future. They characterize the current ECEC landscape as a "state of emergency" (one compounded by the overlapping crises brought about by the COVID-19 pandemic), whose devastating effects have been borne disproportionately by minoritized children, families, and communities. They critically explore the multicultural underpinnings of policies that offer surface-level conceptions of equity, inclusion, and diversity while often omitting any deeper discussion of race and racism. The authors draw on critical race theory to effectively decentre the myth of diversity as a site of national unity and strength, and argue that, for racialized, Black, and Indigenous communities, the celebration of diversity systemically acts as a barrier to equity, as income disparities in Ontario continue to widen along racial lines.

In chapter 2, Alana Butler outlines the various challenges encountered by low-income racialized children and families attempting to access affordable child care. Butler highlights recent funding cuts implemented by the current Progressive Conservative government in Ontario that further marginalize families through spatial inaccessibility, as poorer areas lack high-quality care options. Furthermore, cutbacks to the number of families receiving the Ontario Child Care Tax Credit have left many low-income racialized families to depend on unregulated child-care services. Butler critiques Eurocentric ECEC curricular approaches that further disenfranchise low-income families, such as a lack of culturally relevant pedagogy, mistrust of educational institutions among certain communities, and limited representation of Indigenous and racialized communities in early learning sites.

In chapter 3, Nidhi Menon decentres dominant narratives informing how refugees as a social group are constructed as the vulnerable, poverty-stricken, war-torn "other." As the world witnesses an increasing amount of people on the move, the debate over who should be legitimized as a "refugee" instead of a "migrant" has become hotly contested. Looking at refugee children, Menon draws on two common responses from Western nations. The first—that the refugee child needs help or "saving"—serves as a dominant narrative of colonial paternalism. The second conception—that of the troubled refugee child who is damaged and suffering—conjures up psychological-developmental norms that serve to pathologize refugee children within a deficit framework. By contrast, Menon situates refugee children as competent and resilient social actors with agency and self-determination.

In chapter 4, Alana Powell, Lisa Johnston, and Rachel Langford take up a feminist ethics of care approach to shift our conceptual understandings of equity in the Ontario context. While equity is increasingly normalized in policy discourse, equity as a practice has not materialized. The authors consider the inadequacy and ineffectiveness of traditional liberal, moral theories of thinking with equity, as many of these understandings of equity remain centred on equality. By implementing an ethics of care, the authors contend that the various phases of care provide a framework for how equity can be enacted within institutions.

In chapter 5, Lisa Johnston looks at the role of professionalization in early childhood education in Ontario. In 2007, the College of Early Childhood Educators was established in Ontario, officially designating ECEs as licensed professionals (under the designation of registered early childhood educators, or RECEs). However, the professionalization of the ECEC field has not systematically improved working conditions or wages for RECEs. In the neoliberal era of regulations, increased expectations, and increased workloads with less benefits and pay, women, who comprise the majority of ECEs in Ontario, are repeatedly silenced. Johnston incorporates the perspectives and experiences of ECEs in Ontario to discuss the scaling back of educator planning time as a facet of the wider trend toward neoliberalism and developmentalism.

In an attempt to professionalize the field of ECEC, efforts have been made to "masculinize" it. In chapter 6, Adam Davies and Rhea Ashley Hoskin utilize femme theory and the feminist ethics of care in order to interrogate the ways in which femininity and feminine qualities are devalued, and how this in turn informs how ECEC as a field is devalued. These theories are taken up by the authors as a way to rethink efforts to masculinize the field, and to better understand how they might inform discourses and practices of professionalism in ECEC.

One of the 94 Calls to Action of the Truth and Reconciliation Commission of Canada (2015) seeks the development of culturally appropriate curriculum in early childhood education. In chapter 7, Maya-Rose Simon outlines the impact of colonial education, in the past as well as the present, on Indigenous Peoples in Canada, reviews early childhood education programs in Indigenous communities, and provides an overview of Indigenous knowledge and land-based pedagogy. Simon, a member of the Anishinaabe, Chippewa Nation, and Métis, discusses a research project she undertook exploring how an urban child-care centre might make space, physically, spiritually, and psychologically, for Indigenous knowledge. Through action research, Simon was able to investigate how Indigenous concepts of relationality affected the way one preschool room gathered.

In chapter 8, Maria Karmiris considers the possibilities engendered by the failure and loss of the normative neoliberal subject. Karmiris explores intersectionalities of race, gender, socio-economic status, and disability to imagine new possibilities of teaching and learning that go beyond rigid neoliberal conformity. Karmiris views early childhood education as a site of opportunity where educators and students can turn away from and resist normative trajectories and ideologies and offer new orientations of relationships between and with teaching and learning.

Finally, in chapter 9, Kerry-Ann Escayg views the white racial socialization processes that racialized children undergo in early learning spaces through an anti-Black-racism framework. Escayg outlines the genealogy of Canada's oppressive history, which has often been

perpetuated by educational institutions, and asks practitioners to consider their own teaching practices in relation to their work with Black,
Indigenous, and other racialized students, families, and communities.
In particular, Escayg calls on educators to engage in anti-racist and
self-reflective practices by providing prompts that encourage them to
unpack their own positionalities, interactions, stereotypes, and preconceived notions.

*Equity as Praxis in Early Childhood Education and Care* calls on you,
the reader, to actively engage with the content presented here by critically examining your own social location and positionalities of privilege and oppression as situated in your personal and ancestral histories.
The volume further encourages you to think about your own ideas and
notions of children and childhood, to consider what social factors and
forces inform these images and ideas, and to envision how children
and childhood can be re-imagined to improve ECEC. The authors,
as a collective, call on practitioners, students, and academics alike to
(un)learn, relearn, disrupt, resist, and subvert exclusively psychological-
developmentalist norms that dominate depictions of childhood and
early learning pedagogies and epistemologies via the alternative approaches discussed throughout this text. By considering and critiquing
your own understandings of children, families, communities, and practices in ECEC, the text seeks to provide an alternative strength-based
approach to critical and transformative praxis. This can only be done via
"reflection and action upon the world in order to transform it" (Freire,
1970, p. 51).

Systemic change begins at the micro, grassroots level; it depends on
the emancipation of the mind, followed by a revolution within the heart.
This must be attended by struggle, resiliency, and sacrifice as individuals
and organizations take action, in solidarity with communities, to centre
equity as a sustainable priority for institutional policies and practices
and to reflect the needs of vulnerable identities and communities. We
need to pay attention to social groups who have been marginalized, silenced, and oppressed throughout history. As Freire (2000) reminds us,
"there is no such thing as freedom without risk" (p. 87). Similarly, bell
hooks (2003) in *Teaching Community: A Pedagogy of Hope* emphasizes,

"love in the classroom prepares teachers and students to open our minds and hearts.... Love will always move us away from domination in all its forms. Love will always challenge and change us" (p. 137). Canada's dominant narrative as a "multicultural" society is being complicated, and rightfully so, by the growing recognition that the country has its own dark history of anti-Black and anti-Indigenous racism and other oppressive practices that have systemically disadvantaged racialized and minoritized identities and communities.

(Taking a deep breath).

> Black Lives Matter.
> Indigenous Lives Matter.
>    Muslim Lives Matter.
> Early Childhood Educators Matter.
> Children and Families Matter.
>    Equity is not equality.
> Equality is sameness. Equity is fairness.
> Equity matters!
> Equity has to be action-oriented!

As bell hooks (2001) put it in *All about Love*, "the inability to connect with others carries with it an inability to assume responsibility for causing pain" (p. 39). All of us, to various degrees and capacities, simultaneously contribute to other people's pain and help mitigate and heal these same wounds.

In community, we heal, love, and harness our anger and frustration in search of a better future and to improve the conditions in ECEC. In hope, we continue marching forward, challenging inequity and injustice in its various forms and practices. Along the way, we will reflect, regroup, and re-strategize as necessary in the hope that these efforts have the potential to radically transform ECEC in Canada. We recognize that doing the work of equity goes beyond theory and legislation. It is a daily practice that encompasses the mind, spirit, soul, and heart.

Let us embrace the struggle, pay homage to the past advocates, and hope for a better future. As West and Ritz (2009) emphasize, "the true measure of your humanity will always rest upon the depth of your love and the quality of your service to others" (p. 246). With reflection and action in solidarity, we can and will do better in our praxis. It is a lifetime journey.

In love and community, we heal, hope, and take action.

*Zuhra Abawi*
*Ardavan Eizadirad*
*Rachel Berman*

## REFERENCES

Abawi, Z., & Berman, R. (2019). Politicizing early childhood education and care in Ontario: Race, identity and belonging. *Journal of Curriculum, Teaching, Learning and Leadership in Education, 2*(2), 4–13.

Aboud, F. E. (1988). *Children and prejudice.* Basil Blackwell.

Beach, J., & Ferns, C. (2015). From childcare market to childcare system. *Our Schools, Our Selves, 24*(4), 43–62. https://www.policyalternatives.ca/sites/default/files/uploads/publications/National%20Office/2015/09/OS120_Summer2015_Child_Care_Market_to_Child_Care_System.pdf

Berman, R., & Abawi, Z. (2019). Thinking and doing otherwise: Reconceptualist contributions to early childhood education and care. In S. Jagger (Ed.), *History and philosophy of early years education and care: Canadian perspectives* (pp. 160–195). Canadian Scholars.

Berman, R., Daniel, B. J., Butler, A., MacNevin, M., & Royer, N. (2017). Nothing or almost nothing to report: Early childhood educators and discursive constructions of colourblindness. *International Critical Childhood Policy Studies Journal, 6*(1), 52–65.

Bloch, M. N., Swadener, B. B., & Cannella, G. (2018). *Reconceptualizing early childhood education and care—A reader: Critical questions, new imaginaries and social activism* (2nd ed.). Peter Lang.

Bonilla-Silva, E. (2006). *Racism without the racists? Colorblind racism and the persistence of racial inequality in America* (4th ed.). Rowman & Littlefield.

Brown, S., Souto-Manning, M., & Tropp Laman, T. (2010). Seeing the strange in the familiar: Unpacking racialized practices in early childhood settings. *Race Ethnicity and Education, 13*(4), 513–532.

Butler, A., Teasley, C., & Sánchez-Blanco, C. (2019). A decolonial and intersectional approach to disrupting whiteness, neoliberalism, and patriarchy in Western early childhood education. In P. Trifonas (Ed.), *Handbook of theory and research in cultural studies and education* (pp. 1–18). Springer.

Colour of Poverty. (n.d.). *Colour of poverty factsheets—2019.* Retrieved January 21, 2021, from https://colourofpoverty.ca/fact-sheets/

Eizadirad, A. (2019). Inequality of opportunity: Experiences of racialized and minoritized students. In *Decolonizing educational assessment: Ontario elementary students and the EQAO* (pp. 41–63). Palgrave Macmillan.

Eizadirad, A., & Portelli, J. (2018). Subversion in education: Common misunderstandings and myths. *International Journal of Critical Pedagogy, 9*(1), 53–72.

Escayg, K.-A., Berman, R., & Royer, N. (2017). Canadian children and race: Toward an antiracism analysis. *Journal of Childhood Studies, 42*(2), 10–21.

Freire, P. (1970). *Pedagogy of the oppressed.* Continuum International.

Freire, P. (2000). *Pedagogy of freedom: Ethics, democracy, and civic courage.* Rowman & Littlefield.

Friendly, M., & Prabhu, N. (2010). Can early childhood education and care help keep Canada's promise of respect for diversity? Occasional Paper No. 23, Childcare Resource and Research Unit. https://www.childcarecanada.org/sites/default/files/crru_op23_diversity.pdf

Friendly, M., & Prentice, S. (2009). *About Canada: Childcare.* Fernwood.

Grieshaber, S., & Blaise, M. (2019) Making room for more: Complexity, diversity, and the impact of alternative perspectives on early childhood care and education. In C. P. Brown, M. Benson McMullen, & N. File (Eds.), *The Wiley handbook of early childhood care and education* (pp. 617–640).

hooks, b. (2001). *All about love: New visions.* Harper Perennial.

hooks, b. (2003). *Teaching community: A pedagogy of hope.* Routledge.

Husband, T. (2012). "I don't see color": Challenging assumptions about discussing race with young children. *Early Childhood Education Journal, 39*(6), 365–371.

Iannacci, L., & Whitty, P. (2009). *Early childhood curricula: Reconceptualist perspectives.* Brush Education.

James, C. E., & Turner, T. (2017). *Towards race equity in education: The schooling of black students in the Greater Toronto Area.* York University. https://youthrex.com/report/towards-race-equity-in-education-the-schooling-of-black-students-in-the-greater-toronto-area/

Ladson-Billings, G. (1998). Just what is CRT and what's it doing in a nice field like education? *Qualitative Studies in Education, 1*(11), 102–118.

Matias, C. E. (2013). Tears worth telling: Urban teaching and the possibilities of racial justice. *Multicultural Perspectives, 15*(4), 187–193.

Miller, J. P. (2018). *Love and compassion: Exploring their role in education.* University of Toronto Press.

Nxumalo, F., & Brown, C. P. (Eds.). (2019). *Disrupting and countering deficits in early childhood education.* Routledge.

Pacini-Ketchabaw, V., & Prochner, L. W. (2013). *Re-situating Canadian early childhood education.* Peter Lang.

Reyes, G. T. (2019). Pedagogy of and towards decoloniality. In M. A. Peters (Ed.), *Encyclopedia of teacher education.* Springer, Singapore. https://doi.org/10.1007/978-981-13-1179-6_220-1

Richardson, B., Langford, R., Friendly, M., & Rauhala, A. (2013). From choice to change: An analysis of the "choice" discourse in Canada's 2006 federal election. *Contemporary Issues in Early Childhood, 14*(2), 155–167. doi:10.2304/ciec.2013.14.2.155

Statistics Canada. (2017, October 25). *Immigration and ethnocultural diversity: Key results from the 2016 census.* https://www12.statcan.gc.ca/census-recensement/2016/rt-td/imm-eng.cfm

Thobani, S. (2007). *Exalted subjects: Studies in the making of race and nation in Canada.* University of Toronto Press.

Truth and Reconciliation Commission of Canada. (2015). *Truth and Reconciliation Commission of Canada: Calls to action.* Truth and Reconciliation Commission of Canada. https://nctr.ca/assets/reports/Calls_to_Action_English2.pdf

Tuck, E., & Yang, K. W. (2012). Decolonization is not a metaphor. *Decolonization: Indigeneity, Education & Society, 1*(1), 1–40.

United Way Greater Toronto. (2019). *Rebalancing the opportunity equation.* United Way Greater Toronto. https://www.unitedwaygt.org/file/2019_OE_fullreport_FINAL.pdf

West, C., & Ritz, D. (2009). *Living and loving out loud: A memoir.* Hay House.

# CHAPTER 1

# State of Emergency: Mapping Inequities in Early Childhood Education and Care in Canada

*Ardavan Eizadirad and Zuhra Abawi*

## LEARNING OBJECTIVES

- To discuss the encroachment of neoliberalism and the marketization of ECEC in Canada
- To interrogate the intersectionalities of oppression and how inequities are further exacerbated by neoliberal policy indifference to child care
- To consider the feminization of poverty embedded in ECEC
- To raise awareness of structural, systemic, and institutional inequities behind the fragmentation of ECEC in Canada
- To recognize the state of emergency in which ECEC finds itself in Canada, and to encourage action-oriented strategies to mitigate the systemic issues in the field

## INTRODUCTION

We as authors are calling the current state of **inequity** in early childhood education an emergency: a situation that requires urgent attention and investment from multiple levels of government and partnerships with local organizations to create a sustainable national child-care system in which access to high-quality and affordable child care is seen as a human right for everyone and not only a privilege for the wealthy. The social conditions caused by the COVID-19 pandemic, intensified by the closing of schools and child-care centres due to physical-distancing protocols, are not causal factors in the existing inequities in early childhood education and care (ECEC) in Canada. Rather, the COVID-19 pandemic has simply exposed the many ways in which a child-care system shaped by neoliberal market-driven policies has become inequitable. This has resulted in a lack of federal funding, the absence of a national policy, high user fees, increased privatization, poor wages, and ineffective subsidization for low-income and vulnerable families. In turn, this has led to the rise and perpetuation of a child-care system that is unaffordable, inaccessible, and in many cases unsafe for children (Akbari & McCuaig, 2017; Beach & Ferns, 2015; Child Care Advocacy Association of Canada, n.d.; Friendly, 2015; Halfon & Langford, 2015; Preston et al., 2012; Wilson et al., 2018).

Throughout this chapter, we reflect on how far we have come as a profession historically, socially, and politically, and we envision and discuss what needs to change to create a sustainable long-term plan for child care in Canada, one that makes child care more equitable, affordable, accessible, and inclusive. We are calling things as we see them: the current system is in a *state of emergency*; many vulnerable identities and communities are treated as expendable and disposable, and the current system does not care for their most urgent needs (Akbari & McCuaig, 2017). For example, "the highest rates of child poverty are among Indigenous, racialized, and newcomer families" (Wilson et al., 2018, p. 1), and "Toronto has persistently remained the child poverty capital of Canada with 1 in 4 children living in a low-income family" (p. 5). This is unacceptable, and yet this trend is consistent across the Greater Toronto Area.

We must respond with seriousness and urgency to create a more equitable system that reflects the needs of vulnerable identities and communities. We, as scholars who teach and work in ECEC, are angered and frustrated by the lack of investment and progress in the field, even though research has continuously shown the shortcomings of the market-driven system of child care that has become the norm in nearly all of Canada except Quebec (Child Care Advocacy Association of Canada, n.d.; Halfon & Langford, 2015; Time for Childcare for All, 2020). Indeed, not only has the market-driven approach failed to make high-quality child care accessible for all—in fact, it has helped to intensify and further widen the inequities within ECEC (Colour of Poverty, 2019; Friendly, 2015; Oxfam Canada, 2019; United Way Greater Toronto, 2019).

Writing in 2020, we are declaring a state of emergency in ECEC in Canada because many vulnerable identities and communities are left to secure child care on their own. Many parents are forced to stay at home and miss work in order to take care of their children due to high user fees and long waiting lists; in many cases, the alternative is low-cost child-care options that are often affiliated with lower-quality programming and greater risk.

When possible, parents arrange for other family members to take care of their child(ren) so they can return to work. Currently, on a national level, the supply of accessible child-care services does not meet the demand (Akbari & McCuiag, 2017; Time for Childcare for All, 2020). The market-driven nature of the current Canadian child-care system, in alignment with neoliberal discourses that privilege "choice" over equitable access (Eizadirad & Portelli, 2018), tends to disadvantage low-income and vulnerable families who receive moderate subsidization for the high user fees required for access to low-quality, unregulated child care. This market-driven system continues to be ineffective when it comes to increasing child-care supply opportunities or reducing costs for high-quality child care. Instead, it has led to increases in fees, which often far exceed the rate of inflation. To put the numbers into perspective, "median monthly parent fees across Canada for childcare were $761 for infant care, $701 for toddlers and $674 for preschoolers in 2012" (Friendly, 2015, p. 14). "It is important to note that these numbers include Quebec's low fees as part of the calculation. Median monthly fees in Toronto for infants are $1,649, toddlers

$1,375, and preschoolers $1,150. These are the highest in Canada" (Atkinson Centre for Society and Child Development, 2017, p. 8).

These expenses, when calculated over a one-year period, are very troubling, demonstrating the inequitable nature of child-care costs throughout Canada. Hence our declaration of a state of emergency, the goal of which is to bring a sense of urgency to discussions of the current system. According to Oxfam Canada (2019) in a report titled *Who Cares? Why Canada Needs a Public Child Care System*:

> Compared to its OECD peers, Canada comes in lowest in public spending on early childhood education and care spending, at merely 0.3 per cent of the GDP [gross domestic product], which is well below the international benchmark amount of 1 per cent of GDP. (p. 15)

We need to question why creating a child-care system that is affordable, **inclusive**, and equitable for all is not a priority at all levels of government. This is troubling given that investment in the early years yields larger societal benefits in a variety of sectors. According to the *Early Childhood Education Report* (Akbari & McCuiag, 2017), "economic studies calculate the cost-to-benefit ratio from spending on early education at between $2 and $7 returned for every $1 spent, depending on the population studied" (p. 2). The report goes on to emphasize, "ECE is also a highly effective platform for early identification and intervention. By addressing problems early, special education costs are reduced. In a country highly dependent on immigration, early education acts as a settlement program" (p. 2). We need change and we need it now more than ever, both at the micro and macro levels, as we adjust to child care in a post-COVID setting. This is an opportunity to do things differently by placing equity at the heart of the new systemic changes being introduced. But while the federal Liberal government has pledged to invest in a national child-care strategy, tangible steps toward a cohesive, countrywide approach have yet to be initiated at the time of this writing.

## THE ECEC FIELD AND THE FABLE OF THE BOILING FROG

The fable of the boiling frog goes like this: If a frog is thrown into a pot of boiling water, it will jump out immediately. The extreme temperature signals danger to the frog, and it responds by fleeing from it. But if the frog is placed in warm water that is then brought slowly to a boiling temperature, it will not perceive the gradual increase in danger. As the water gradually gets hotter, the threat appears undetectable to the frog, which ultimately leads to its death.

The trajectory of ECEC in Canada has much in common with the fable of the boiling frog. We have gradually arrived at a state of emergency in which families with young children are forced to relocate and sacrifice their careers. It is important to emphasize that these sacrifices predominantly impact women and those belonging to minoritized groups in Canada (Friendly, 2015). Moreover, many families are living paycheque to paycheque in order to afford the expensive user fees affiliated with child care. If we do not react now, many more of our most vulnerable families with young children, particularly Black and Indigenous families, people of colour, 2SLGBTQ+, those from lower socio-economic backgrounds, and children with exceptionalities, will be further disenfranchised by the market-driven system that prioritizes profit over people.

In 2015, a report was drafted in consultation with various child-care policy experts across Canada, titled *Child Care in Canada by 2020: A Vision and a Way Forward*. The report was organized around three principles that aim to make child care across Canada more equitable: universality, high quality, and comprehensiveness. The shortcomings in the field of ECEC outlined in the report included lack of a national ECEC program or policy, lack of investment by the federal government, difficulty retaining qualified early childhood educators due to lack of a regard for the profession and poor wages, high user fees for parents, inaccessibility and long waiting lists for regulated child care, and lack of high-quality programming in unregulated child-care centres. Sadly, the same issues remain in 2020, with only modest improvements.

The ECEC field has long been lacking holistic federal investment via funding and a cohesive national policy framework to make high-quality child care accessible, affordable, and inclusive to all. The marketization and privatization trends encompassing ECEC have led to an inequitable system that is passed down from government to government, election after election. Without a national child-care policy and a guarantee of extensive federal funding regardless of what political party is in power, the harmful impacts of the current system of profit-driven child care cannot be reversed. Noteworthy progress that can guide a new national vision of child care that prioritizes equity includes Quebec's program, which funds services rather than subsidize individual families, and Ontario's expansion of full-day kindergarten programs for all four- and five-year-olds within schools supported by a teacher and an early childhood educator working collaboratively to provide high-quality programming (Child Care Advocacy Association of Canada, n.d.).

## THE HISTORY OF ECEC IN CANADA

Canada, unlike other highly developed nations, lacks an overarching national child-care policy as well as a comprehensive educational strategy. Federal ambitions to draft such a strategy have been minimal, although several attempts to devise such policies have been made. The omission of national educational and child-care initiatives is due in part to Canada's federal constitutional framework. Under the Constitution Act, 1867, the division of powers between provincial and territorial governments and the federal government were enacted (Friendly et al., 2016). Canada's ECEC landscape is often characterized as a "patchwork" model as each province and territory formulates its own child-care initiatives, and these vary drastically in terms of licensing requirements, training, and certification (Friendly et al., 2016). As such, while child-care operations existed across Canada during the early 1900s, there was limited government intervention in such services until the onset of World War Two. In 1942, the Privy Council commissioned the Dominion-Provincial

Wartime Agreement, Canada's only federal child-care framework and the closest the country has come to enacting a national child-care policy. The initiative provided a 50/50 cost-sharing arrangement to help provinces and territories provide child care to mothers who were deemed essential wartime workers.

However, after the war this federal incentive was rescinded and child care once again became an individual responsibility of families (Friendly et al., 2016). In 1966, the Canada Assistance Plan (CAP) was introduced with the aim of reducing poverty by financially assisting low-income families for what was considered "welfare" services, which included child care. The federal government once again offered a 50/50 cost-sharing agreement with the provinces and territories as part of income subsidies. In 1971, out-of-pocket parental expenses toward child care were permitted as tax deductions under the Income Tax Act, and by the mid-1980s, the majority of five-year-olds across the country were enrolled in publicly funded half-day kindergarten programs. Ontario continues to be the only province with universal full-day kindergarten for all four- and five-year-olds, which was rolled out under the Liberal government of Kathleen Wynne in 2014 (Akbari & McCuaig, 2017; Friendly et al., 2016).

Between 1984 and 1995, three more attempts were made to implement a national child-care framework. The first was the Taskforce on Childcare under Pierre Elliott Trudeau in 1984, the second the Special Committee on Childcare introduced by the Brian Mulroney government in 1986, while the third and final attempt was the Red Book election commitment undertaken by Jean Chrétien in 1993. Each of the aforementioned prime ministers recognized the importance of universal child-care incentives; however, none of these initiatives resulted in a national framework. During the mid- to late 1990s, provinces and territories asserted their power and control over their own jurisdictions, and federal powers were significantly weakened. In 1996, the CAP program was eliminated and all federal funding toward public services, including education, health-care, and welfare programs, were consolidated into one collective fund known as the Canada Health and Social Transfer (Friendly, 2015).

It is also important to note that under the Indian Act of 1867, which still exists, the federal government is responsible for services and programs otherwise designated as provincial and territorial responsibilities. However, as part of its 94 Calls to Action, the Truth and Reconciliation Commission (2015) has called for the drafting of a national Indigenous Early Learning and Child Care Framework (Friendly et al., 2016).

Although the calls for a sustainable national child-care policy framework continue to be made, limited political significance has been afforded to such activism. This is in part due to the positioning of ECEC as discursively distinct and separate from K–12 education (more on this in the following section). Methods implemented thus far to reduce astronomical ECEC fees continue to amount to band-aid solutions, whereby funding incentives are provided to individual families as consumers who can then choose their child-care preference, such as the Live-In Caregivers Program, home child care, or centre-based care. These disjointed "choices," rooted as they are in neoliberal discourses, take precedence over collaborative investment in a national framework that would benefit all Canadian children, especially those most marginalized by marketized policy approaches.


## GRADUALLY BOILING THE WATER: RISE OF A MARKET-DRIVEN MODEL OF ECEC FUELLED BY PROFIT AND IGNORING INEQUITIES

Returning to the fable of the boiling frog and the current state of emergency in ECEC, we ask: What are the indicators that the water has gradually been boiling and killing us slowly when it comes to children, parents, early childhood educators (ECEs), practitioners, activists, and others in the ECEC sector? Who is impacted by this emergency and in what ways? More importantly, what factors contribute to the rise and perpetuation of the circumstances constituting a state of emergency?

Although Canada's ECEC arena is classified as a disjointed "patchwork" lacking cohesion among the provinces and territories, there is one form of unity among this patchwork, and that is the discursive constructions of ECEC, which position the field outside of the paradigm of education, and thus as an individual responsibility of families (Langford et al., 2020). The lack of a national child-care policy framework and federal funding for the sector, particularly in the early years prior to kindergarten, have prioritized profit-making at the expense of community needs (Beach & Ferns, 2015; Eizadirad & Portelli, 2018). Across Canada, with the exception of Quebec, the commonality among the patchwork is the commodification of ECEC, a process driven by neoliberal market trends, and which conceptualizes ECEC as a commodity rather than a social and public good (Beach & Ferns, 2015; Bezanson, 2017; Halfon & Langford, 2015).

As we are experiencing a state of emergency in ECEC, it is important to explore how and why child care is discursively characterized as an individual responsibility rather than a public right. In Ontario, where the authors of this chapter are situated, skyrocketing fees for child care have been compounded by a lack of access to regulated child-care spaces. Currently, only 20 percent of the province's child-care facilities are licensed (Kirmse, 2018). While ECEC in Ontario operates as a division of the provincial Ministry of Education, merged under the label "Early ON" as of 2018, it is not publicly funded as part of K–12 education. The off-loading of social-liberal state responsibilities onto individual "consumers," a process aided by narratives privileging consumer "choice," is fuelled by steep governmental budget cuts to social services.

In Ontario, steps have been taken to improve the status of ECEs, particularly with the College of Early Childhood Educators (CECE), which was introduced in 2007 as a regulatory body for the profession. The professionalization narrative in Ontario has been strongly informed by masculinist, racist, and capitalist discourses entrenched in the Progressive Conservative Party of Ontario's conceptions of feminized labour and care work (Abawi et al., 2019). ECEC in the Canadian context cannot be divorced from its positionality within the gendered, racialized, and hetero-patriarchal power relations through which Canada as a settler-colonial state operates (Tuck & Yang, 2012). The overwhelming majority of ECEs are women, with some studies placing them as high as 97 percent of the workforce (Bezanson, 2017). The **intersectionalities** of race, gender, and socio-economic status inform the very structures that devalue care work and bring about poor working conditions and wages, high turnover rates, and limited opportunities for professional growth among ECEs. At the same time, ECEs have increased expectations for engagement with professional-development activities as a result of their status as members of CECE (Abawi et al., 2019).

Women and children are thus marginalized throughout Canada by the privileging of neoliberal profit ambitions over the public and social good. When considering the **feminization of poverty**, we must draw holistically from the intersectional nature of various positionalities to contemplate racialized and feminized poverty. It is important to note that when we use the term *racialized*, we are referring to people of non-European heritage, regardless of whether or not they are born in Canada (Abawi & Eizadirad, 2020). According to Statistics Canada (2017), 20.8 percent of racialized people live in poverty compared to 12.2 percent of non-racialized people. Moreover, 80 percent of Indigenous people live in poverty. Additionally, Indigenous and racialized bodies are disproportionately employed in **precarious work** affiliated with low-paying, part-time, and often temporary contract work with few or no benefits (Evans & Gibb, 2009). Racialized women are 48 percent more likely to be unemployed than white men, and those racialized women who are employed earn a fraction—a mere 55.6 percent—of what white men earn (Block & Galabuzi, 2011). The indicators of precarious employment characterize the working conditions of many ECEs, including those employed by Catholic and public school boards in Ontario's full-day kindergarten program, positions that are often coveted due to their higher hourly wages (Association of Early Childhood Educators Ontario, 2016; Gananathan, 2015). However, ECEs working in publicly funded school boards are laid off during the summer months and must apply for employment insurance, while elementary teachers do not. Many ECEs also take on split shifts and commute between different school sites, which means they are denied planning time to program for the needs of their learners (Johnston, 2019). Moreover, ECEs are increasingly likely to encounter the residual implications of precarious work, notably illness, burnout, mental health issues, and injury (Association of Early Childhood Educators Ontario, 2016, 2018). The positioning of women within the national discourse as natural caregivers and substitute mothers (Bezanson, 2017; Moss, 2006) has further devalued and gendered labour force participation among Canadian women, who must choose between employment or remaining at home to look after their own children (Richardson et al., 2013). As professors who have taught ECE courses in a degree program at a large post-secondary institution, many of our students shared concerns about the devaluation of their field; some students' peers and family members even referred to them as "glorified babysitters."

The United Nations Children's Fund (UNICEF) placed Canada last with Ireland in terms of access to quality ECEC among industrial nations (UNICEF, 2008). Additionally, the Organisation for Economic Co-operation and Development (OECD) cited a lack of affordable child care across Canada, noting that Canadian families pay significantly more than their OECD counterparts. In Toronto, as mentioned earlier, the average monthly cost of child care is $1,649 for infants, $1,375 for toddlers, and $1,150 for preschoolers (Akbari & McCuaig, 2017). However, the average wage for ECEs across Ontario is $17 per hour (Association of Early Childhood Educators Ontario, 2018). Quebec presents a sharp contrast with Ontario, since parent fees are approximately $183 per month thanks to a universal child-care service program enacted in Quebec in 1996.

In 2010, Prince Edward Island took steps to universalize ECEC programs, and, in 2018, British Columbia's $10-per-day child-care centres were underway (Friendly et al., 2016; Langford et al., 2017). Parental out-of-pocket fees are significantly lower in Quebec, Prince Edward Island, and Manitoba, where provincial governments set capped parent fees for child care. However, all cities across Canada (excluding those in Quebec and Winnipeg, Manitoba) had parent fees that exceeded $700 per month (Friendly et al., 2016). The consumer model of financing child care, in conjunction with neoliberal choice discourses (Friendly & Prentice, 2009; Richardson et al., 2013), constructs parents as consumers who ought to be afforded "choice" when shopping for access to child care. Such options include home child care, centre-based child care, live-in care, and for-profit and not-for-profit child care. Rather than a federal public child-care investment strategy, funding is dispersed through initiatives such as the Canada Child Tax Benefit, which goes to families who then choose from the array of aforementioned services, many of which are unregulated and of low quality (Beach & Ferns, 2015).

In addition to high costs for child care in the early years, child-care services are planned and arranged in a way that prioritizes the bottom line, rather than community and social needs (Beach & Ferns, 2015). Many rural and Indigenous communities therefore lack access to child-care services and resources due to discursive practices that place ECEC outside of the realm of education. The absence of a cohesive federal policy can be seen in policy neglect, cutbacks, limited growth of regulated spaces, and increasing privatization. Further, curriculum programming is used as a marketing strategy whereby school readiness takes precedence over other holistic models for growth and learning, including Indigenous epistemologies and other "centric" pedagogical approaches (Dei, 2006; Sanford et al., 2012). As Sanford et al. (2012) beautifully articulate,

> Schooling [with which we include early years programming and services] influenced and shaped by neoliberalist discourse—valuing linear over cyclical progression, competition over collaboration, dualism over complexity, and product over process—is exclusionary and does not accommodate the learning needs of many students. It does not take into account the diversity of students in 21st century society in relation to culture, race, gender, sexual orientation, economic potential, disability, or beliefs. (p. 20)

We can and must do better in Canada, on both a systemic and an individual level. Where do we begin?

## DYING SLOWLY FROM LACK OF CHOICE, INACCESSIBILITY, AND INEQUITIES

Overall, we have discussed and identified the following factors contributing to the rise and normalization of a profit-driven and inequitable child-care system in Canada:

- Lack of a national policy to guide a long-term sustainable plan for affordable and high-quality child care for all
- Lack of long-term funding irrespective of what government or political party is in power
- Increases in user fees for parents
- Lack of access to high-quality child care affiliated with long waiting lists
- Normalization of neoliberal government policies affiliated with the subsidization of parent fees driven by profit instead of community needs
- Supply not meeting demand nationally
- Devaluation and feminization of care work as a profession
- Feminization of poverty: families, particularly those led by women, have to choose between going back to their careers or staying at home to take care of their children
- Poor wages for ECEs, who also lack of benefits and institutional support
- High turnover rates for ECEs, with many leaving the profession for teaching jobs, in which they make double the salary and obtain job security and benefits

## CONCLUSION

If Canada wants to improve the conditions in ECEC—and save the boiling frog—it needs to stop being short-sighted and instead invest in and implement a sustainable long-term plan aimed at mitigating the inequities that currently exist and are harming many vulnerable identities and communities. According to Oxfam Canada (2019), Canada spends a mere 0.3 percent of its GDP on child care; this is the lowest public expenditure among its OECD peers, the benchmark being 1 percent. In Nordic countries such as Sweden and Denmark, by comparison, "public expenditure on early childhood services is equivalent to about 2% of GDP" (Moss, 2006, p. 33). Our most vulnerable identities and communities cannot continue to be treated as expendable and disposable, nor can profit continue to take precedence over basic human needs such as access to quality and affordable child care in the early years. We need to recognize that every child matters. We need to treat present circumstances as what they are: a state of emergency. Currently, "child poverty rates in Canada are 13% for White non-immigrant children, but 51% for Indigenous children (and 60% for Indigenous children living on reserve); 32% for children of immigrants; and 25% for children of colour when taken as a whole" (Colour of Poverty, 2019, p. 2).

We must reflect on the past and strategize, collectively and in solidarity, to take immediate action to create a more equitable child-care system that offers affordable, high-quality programming. This is, after all, a human right and not just a privilege for the wealthy.

To this end we would like to consider some positive teachable moments on which we could build:

- Regions that have merged school programs and child care, which allows more mothers to work, creates full-time employment for educators, and reduces transitions for children
- Quebec's child-care program, which funds services rather than subsidizing individual families
- Ontario's gradual implementation of full-day kindergarten, in which ECEs and teachers work collaboratively to educate four- and five-year-olds through high-quality programs and services

As we reflect on the lessons learned and develop more effective reform actions to mitigate the conditions of our current state of emergency in ECEC, we reiterate and emphasize the recommendations made by the Affordable Child Care for All Plan (Time for Childcare for All, 2020). Created in consultation with various experts and practitioners, the plan aims to build a universal child-care system by 2030. To this end, it calls for the Government of Canada to

- Play a greater leadership role in building a stable child-care system for all over the next 10 years through various bilateral agreements
- Boost funding significantly by increasing Canada's ELCC (Early Learning and Child Care) budget by $1 billion each year over 10 years to meet international benchmarks and reach the goal of affordable, high-quality, and inclusive child care for all across Canada
- Negotiate with the provinces and territories ELCC agreements that demand action on three fronts simultaneously:
  a. Planned expansion of public/non-profit services
  b. Making child care affordable through operational funding and set fees
  c. Improving quality and stability through public spending on the child-care workforce, including improving child-care-sector wages
- Continue to work with Indigenous leaders and communities to operationalize, implement, and expand on the Indigenous Early Learning and Child Care Framework to realize the goals and aspirations of Indigenous Peoples
- Put in place federal infrastructure (legislation, a federal secretariat, funding to the child-care sector) to support the implementation of the plan (p. 2)

The road map for change is in our hands. It's time to take action with urgency, care, and intentionality.

## CRITICAL THINKING QUESTIONS

1. In the context of early childhood education, do you find the analogy of the boiling frog helpful? Why or why not?
2. Were you aware that Canada lacks a national child-care or education strategy? If so, what surprises you the most?
3. Do you believe that Quebec's ECEC plan can be employed as a road map for the rest of Canada? What would be some challenges for such implementation?

## GLOSSARY OF KEY TERMS

**feminization of poverty:** Women are much more likely than men to live in poverty and earn low wages. The feminization of poverty arises due to barriers that prevent women from fully accessing and participating in the labour market. This of course also differs according to intersectionality; for example, racialized and Indigenous women are disproportionately more likely to live in poverty than their white counterparts.

**inclusive:** All individuals, regardless of their identities, are able to access resources, such as high-quality education and care.

**inequity:** Discrepancies that occur beyond right and/or wrong or fair and/or unfair, and which occur due to societal power imbalances—having to do with such things as race, gender, sexual orientation, (dis)ability, nationality, religion—that impact access to resources.

**intersectionalities:** Identities are fluid and encompass many intersecting positionalities (such as race and gender) and inform the individual's daily lived experiences and access to resources in dominant society.

**precarious work:** Non-standard employment arrangement characterized by one or more of the following: low wages, lack of benefits, unstable contract (lack of permanence), poor working conditions.

## REFERENCES

Abawi, Z., Berman, R., & Powell, A. (2019). Gender, race and precarity: Theorizing the parallels between early childhood educators and contract faculty in Ontario. *Atlantis: Critical Studies in Gender, Culture and Social Justice, 40*(1), 45–60.

Abawi, Z., & Eizadirad, A. (2020). Bias-free or biased hiring? Racialized teachers' perspectives on educational hiring practices in Ontario. *Canadian Journal of Educational Administration and Policy, 193*, 18–31.

Akbari, E., & McCuaig, K. (2017). *Early childhood education report.* Atkinson Centre for Society and Child Development at the Ontario Institute for Studies in Education/University of Toronto. http://ecereport.ca/media/uploads/2017-report-pdfs/ece-report2017-en-feb6.pdf

Association of Early Childhood Educators Ontario. (2016). *"I'm more than 'just'
an ECE": Decent work from the perspective of Ontario's early childhood workforce*.
Association of Early Childhood Educators Ontario. https://www.childcarecanada
.org/sites/default/files/Im%20more%20than%20just%20an%20ECE.pdf

Association of Early Childhood Educators Ontario. (2018, January 19). *AECEO
Pre-budget submission*. https://d3n8a8pro7vhmx.cloudfront.net/aeceo/
pages/2325/attachments/original/1517434530/AECEO_2018_Pre-budget_
submission.pdf?1517434530

Atkinson Centre for Society and Child Development. (2017). *Trends in ECEC from
2011–2017*. http://ecereport.ca/media/uploads/2017-profiles-updated/on_final-
feb14.pdf

Beach, J., & Ferns, C. (2015). From childcare market to childcare system. *Our
Schools, Our Selves, 24*(4), 43–62. https://www.policyalternatives.ca/sites/default/
files/uploads/publications/National%20Office/2015/09/OS120_Summer2015_
Child_Care_Market_to_Child_Care_System.pdf

Bezanson, K. (2017). Mad Men social policy: Families, social reproduction, and
childcare in a conservative Canada. In R. Langford, S. Prentice, & P. Albanese
(Eds.), *Caring for children: Social movements and public policy in Canada*
(pp. 19–37). UBC Press.

Block, S., & Galabuzi, G. (2011). *Canada's colour coded labour market: The gap for
racialized workers*. Canadian Centre for Policy Alternatives. https://www
.wellesleyinstitute.com/wp-content/uploads/2011/03/Colour_Coded_Labour_
MarketFINAL.pdf

Child Care Advocacy Association of Canada. (n.d.). *Child care in Canada by 2020: A
vision and a way forward*. Retrieved January 21, 2021, from https://ccaacacpsge.
wordpress.com/child-care-by-2020-a-vision-and-a-way-forward/

Colour of Poverty. (2019). *Fact sheet #3: Racialized poverty in education & learning*.
https://colourofpoverty.ca/wp-content/uploads/2019/03/cop-coc-fact-sheet-3-
racialized-poverty-in-education-learning-3.pdf

Dei, G. S. (2006). We cannot be colour blind: Race, antiracism and the subversion of
dominant thinking. In E. W. Ross (Ed.), *Race, ethnicity, and education: Racism
and antiracism in education* (Vol. 4, pp. 25–42). Praeger.

Eizadirad, A., & Portelli, J. (2018). Subversion in education: Common
misunderstandings & myths. *International Journal of Critical Pedagogy, 9*(1),
53–72.

Evans, J., & Gibb, E. (2009). *Moving from precarious employment to decent work.* Global Union Research Network International Labour Office. Trade Union Advisory Committee to the Organisation for Economic Co-operation and Development, Discussion Paper 13.

Friendly, M. (2015). Taking Canada's child care pulse: The state of ECEC in 2015. *Our Schools Our Selves, 24*(4), 7–24. https://www.policyalternatives.ca/sites/default/files/uploads/publications/National%20Office/2015/09/OS120_Summer2015_Canadas_child_care_pulse.pdf

Friendly, M., Larsen, E., Feltham, L., Grady, B., Forer, B., & Jones, M. (2016). *Early childhood education and care in Canada 2016.* Childcare Resource and Research Unit. https://www.childcarecanada.org/sites/default/files/ECEC-in-Canada-2016.pdf

Friendly, M., & Prentice, S. (2009). *About Canada: Childcare.* Fernwood.

Gananathan, R. (2015). Implications of full day kindergarten program policy on early childhood pedagogy and practice. *International Journal of Child Care and Education Policy, 5*(2), 33–45.

Halfon, S., & Langford, R. (2015). Developing and supporting a high quality child care workforce in Canada. What are the barriers to change? *Our Schools, Our Selves, 24*(4), 131–143.

Johnston, L. (2019). *Dangerous time: A critical qualitative inquiry into ECEs' perspectives on planning time in Southern Ontario* [Unpublished master's thesis]. Ryerson University.

Kirmse, N. (2018, May 23). Analysis: Daycare fees continue to rise across Canada. *CTV News.* https://www.ctvnews.ca/features/analysis-daycare-fees-continue-to-rise-across-canada-1.3940099

Langford, R., Albanese, P., Bezanson, K., Prentice, S., Richardson, B., Banks, M., & Powell, A. (2017). Caring about care: A closer look at care in Canadian childcare—project bulletin #1. https://www.oise.utoronto.ca/atkinson/UserFiles/File/Resources_Topics/Stuff/Caring_about_Care_Project_Bulletin_1.pdf

Langford, R., Powell, A., & Bezanson, K. (2020). Imagining a caring early childhood education and care system in Canada: A thought experiment. *International Journal of Care and Caring, 4*(1), 105–115.

Moss, P. (2006). Structures, understandings and discourses: Possibilities for re-envisioning the early childhood worker. *Contemporary Issues in Early Childhood, 7*(1), 30–41.

Oxfam Canada. (2019). *Who cares? Why Canada needs a public child care system.* Oxfam Canada. https://42kgab3z3i7s3rm1xf48rq44-wpengine.netdna-ssl.com/wp-content/uploads/2019/05/who-cares-report-WEB_EN.pdf

Preston, J. P., Cottrell, M., Pelletier, T. R., & Pearce, J. V. (2012). Aboriginal early childhood education in Canada: Issues of context. *Journal of Early Childhood Research, 10*(1), 3–18.

Richardson, B., Langford, R., Friendly, M., & Rahaula, A. (2013). From choice to change: An analysis of the "choice" discourse in Canada's 2006 federal election. *Contemporary Issues in Early Childhood, 14*(2), 155–167.

Sanford, K., Williams, L., Hopper, T., & McGregor, C. (2012). Indigenous principles decolonizing teacher education: What we have learned. *In Education, 18*(2), 18–34.

Statistics Canada. (2017, October 25). *Ethnic and cultural origins of Canadians: Portrait of a rich heritage.* http://www12.statcan.gc.ca/census-recensement/2016/as-sa/98-200-x/2016016/98-200-x2016016-eng.cfm

Time for Childcare for All. (2020). The affordable child care for all plan. https://timeforchildcare.ca/wp-content/uploads/2019/03/child-care-for-all-plan-FINAL-EN.pdf

Truth and Reconciliation Commission of Canada. (2015). *Truth and Reconciliation Commission of Canada: Calls to action.* Truth and Reconciliation Commission of Canada. http://trc.ca/assets/pdf/Calls_to_Action_English2.pdf

Tuck, E., & Yang, K. W. (2012). Decolonization is not a metaphor. *Decolonization: Indigeneity, Education & Society, 1*(1), 1–40.

UNICEF. (2008). *The child care transition, Innocenti Report Card 8.* UNICEF Innocenti Research Centre. https://www.unicef-irc.org/publications/pdf/rc8_eng.pdf

United Way Greater Toronto. (2019). *Rebalancing the opportunity equation.* United Way Greater Toronto. https://www.unitedwaygt.org/file/2019_OE_fullreport_FINAL.pdf

Wilson, B., Maddox, R., Polanyi, M., Kerr, M., Ekra, M., & Khanna, A. (2018). *2018 Toronto child & family poverty report: Municipal election edition.* Social Planning Toronto. https://d3n8a8pro7vhmx.cloudfront.net/socialplanningtoronto/pages/2079/attachments/original/1538147211/2018_Child_Family_Poverty_Report_Municipal_Election_Edition.pdf?1538147211

CHAPTER 2

# Low-Income Racialized Children and Access to Quality ECEC in Ontario

*Alana Butler*

## LEARNING OBJECTIVES

- To discuss and identify the barriers that low-income racialized children and families face when attempting to access high-quality ECEC programs
- To describe the theories of colour-blind racism and intersectionality
- To explore the strategies that educators and policy-makers can use to support low-income racialized children and their families

## INTRODUCTION

Given the lack of universal child care in Canada, low-income racialized children and their families face many barriers to high-quality early childhood education and care (ECEC) programs. This chapter outlines three main barriers in Ontario. The first is financial: as a result of high costs, many low-income parents and guardians choose unregulated child care that is of much lower quality and may even pose physical dangers (White et al., 2019). The second is spatial: studies of spatial accessibility show that low-income areas lack local access to a range of child-care and health services (Shah et al., 2016). Many low-income families must rely on public transportation or walk long distances to access local child care, and low-income racialized parents who are recent immigrants or refugees face linguistic barriers that may affect their ability to apply for financial subsidies or identify local early childhood education (ECE) resources. And the third is cultural and racial: the Eurocentric nature of early years curriculum and the lack of culturally relevant ECEC pedagogy act as barriers for low-income racialized and Indigenous children. These children are less likely to see themselves represented in the curriculum, and when they experience racism it is most often unreported (Berman et al., 2017).

Children in ECEC settings in Ontario are becoming more racially and culturally diverse. In the 2016 Canadian census, 3.8 million Ontarians, representing 29.3 percent of the province's total population (Statistics Canada, 2017b), identified themselves as members of **racialized** groups. Between 2011 and 2016, the number of Ontario residents who identified themselves as members of racialized groups grew by 18.5 percent (Statistics Canada, 2017b).

According to the 2016 census, there were 7,540,830 foreign-born individuals in Canada, representing over one-fifth (21.9 percent) of the country's total population. Ontarians reported over 250 ethnic origins in the 2016 census (Statistics Canada, 2017b). Ontario has the largest population of any province in Canada, and most immigrants choose Ontario as their destination of choice. Ontario received 39 percent of recent immigrants to Canada in 2016 (Statistics Canada, 2017b). The majority—61 percent—of all immigrants and refugees to Canada settle in Toronto, Montreal, or Vancouver. The four largest visible minority groups in Ontario are South Asian, Chinese, Black, and Filipino. These groups account for almost 75 percent of all visible minorities in Ontario (Statistics Canada, 2017b). Ontario's fastest-growing population is Indigenous. Data from the 2016 census indicates that the province is home to about 375,000 individuals who identify as Indigenous, representing almost 3 percent of the total population (Statistics Canada, 2017b). From 2011 to 2016, the Indigenous population in Ontario grew

23 percent faster than the non-Indigenous population. More Indigenous people are choosing to identify themselves than they did in the past because of recent legislation and the Truth and Reconciliation Commission (Statistics Canada, n.d.).

Linguistic diversity is increasing in Canada as well. Almost 7.6 million Canadians speak a language other than French or English at home, representing an increase of 1 million people since 2011 (Statistics Canada, 2017b). In the 2016 census, Ontarians reported about 200 different mother tongues. The most common mother tongue is Chinese (Mandarin and Cantonese), representing almost 5 percent of the Ontario population. The next most frequently spoken languages include Italian, Punjabi, Spanish, and Arabic. The fastest-growing languages include Arabic, Hindi, Persian, Bengali, Urdu, and Tagalog (Statistics Canada, 2017b).

This demographic diversity brings with it demands for access to high-quality early learning and care. Researchers have defined high-quality early learning as safe, accessible, affordable, and fully integrated to include stable financing and critical pedagogy (Child Care Advocacy Association of Canada, n.d.; Friendly, 2015; Friendly & Prentice, 2009; Halfon & Langford, 2015). Quality early learning and care involves highly trained ECE professionals with post-secondary education (Friendly, 2015; Friendly & Prentice, 2009). In addition, quality ECEC services should offer a variety of options for full- and part-time centres, emergency/respite care, regulated home care, and parenting support programs (Child Care Advocacy Association of Canada, n.d.; Friendly, 2015; Halfon & Langford, 2015). Lastly, quality early learning should provide decent wages and stable employment for registered early childhood educators (ECEs) (Association of Early Childhood Educators Ontario, 2017). A 2017 report by the Association of Early Childhood Educators Ontario (AECEO) points out that the majority of early childhood educators earn little more than the minimum wage, with an average of $17 per hour. The AECEO proposes to raise this wage to a minimum of $25 per hour. The AECEO policy documents link low wages to higher turnover, poorer-quality teaching, and reduced incentives to upgrade one's teaching skills (AECEO, 2017).

In this chapter, I argue that **low-income** racialized families face barriers to high-quality early childhood education and care. The barriers are financial, spatial, and cultural and racial. The chapter first outlines the theoretical approach taken, then provides an analysis of the aforementioned barriers, and concludes with a discussion and recommendations.

## THEORETICAL FRAMEWORK

This chapter draws on the theoretical framework of **colour-blind racism** (Bonilla-Silva, 2014) and intersectionality theory (Crenshaw, 1991). Bonilla-Silva (2014) defined colour-blind racism as a dominant racial ideology in which race is deemed to be unimportant while racial inequality is simultaneously (and paradoxically) perpetuated in society. This definition of colour-blind racism provides a means to understand the absence of racial discourses within early childhood education and care. Studies have found that early learning policies and practices are framed around colour-blindness (Berman et al., 2017; Butler et al., 2019; Husband, 2010, 2012; Morgan, 2010). The four frames of colour-blind racism are abstract liberalism, naturalization, cultural racism, and minimization of racism (Bonilla-Silva, 2014). Abstract liberalism is centred around individualism and equality but does not address equity. Naturalization is the position that racism is natural and not a consequence of socialization. Cultural racism accounts for racial inequalities by attributing its causes to cultural differences rather than structural ones. Lastly, minimization refers to the idea that racism no longer has a significant impact on individual lives. Each of these frames functions collectively to minimize the salience of race and the social consequence of racial inequities (Bonilla-Silva, 2014).

The racialization of poverty can be explored through an intersectional lens that examines how race, gender, and class form interlocking oppressions. Theorists of **intersectionality** assert that race, gender, class, and sexuality cannot be separated from one's identity (Collins, 2000; Crenshaw, 1991). This approach offers a lens through which we can examine the experiences of low-income racialized families in Ontario. These families encounter systems of oppression that may include anti-Black racism, Islamophobia, homophobia, transphobia, classism, sexism, and ageism in a society whose dominant culture is white, heterosexual, and middle-class. These two theoretical approaches are key to analyzing how low-income racialized populations experience early childhood education.

In May 2020, an unarmed African-American male named George Floyd was murdered by a white police officer. The events were captured on video, and the aftermath generated local and global protests against anti-Black racism and policing. In Ontario, local chapters of Black Lives Matter organized many protests against the dozens of murders of unarmed Black Canadians in police encounters (Martinez-Lopez, 2020). These incidents have drawn global attention to the persistence of anti-Black racism, and they also challenge notions of colour-blindness, both of which are perpetuated in the early years.

## BARRIERS TO QUALITY ECEC FOR LOW-INCOME RACIALIZED FAMILIES

### Financial Barriers

In Ontario, the average per-child monthly cost for full-time child care ranges from $900 to $1,600, depending on the region (Financial Accountability Office of Ontario, 2019). Child-care spaces are extremely limited, and parents have to spend months on waiting lists to access public child care. In Canada, there is no universal access to quality early learning and care (Friendly, 2015). In 2018, the Ontario Liberal government under Kathleen Wynne proposed free licensed daycare for preschool-aged children from the age of two and a half until kindergarten beginning in 2020 and over 3,000 additional child care spaces (Office of the Premier, 2018). After a Conservative government was elected in 2018, this proposed policy was eliminated in favour of the Child-care Access and Relief from Expenses tax credit. While tax credits are beneficial for some, the benefits of free and universal quality child care

are significant for a broader segment of the population, and especially for low-income families. Tax credits do not provide spaces or guarantee access to quality early learning and care. Ferns and Beach (2015) argue that the current market-driven approach to early childhood education and care supports for-profit models that may be detrimental to low-income families. For-profit centres are more expensive, provide only the minimal staffing numbers to be profitable, may hire ECEs who are not as well trained, and provide fewer supports for children with exceptionalities.

In 2016, there were 4.8 million Canadians living in a low-income household, nearly one-quarter of whom were children (Statistics Canada, 2017a). Nearly 1.2 million of 6.8 million children in Canada live in a low-income household (Statistics Canada, 2017a). Low-income households are defined as those with incomes lower than the **LICO (Low-Income Cut Off)** for each year and region (Statistics Canada, 2017a). Statistics Canada (2015) defines LICO as "income thresholds below which a family will likely devote a larger share of its income on the necessities of food, shelter and clothing than the average family" ("What are the LICOs?" section).

Preschool children are more vulnerable to poverty because new mothers' earnings decrease during the year of childbirth and the first few years of their children's lives because of reduced pay, part-time employment, or withdrawal from the workforce (Statistics Canada, 2017a). The data shows that 18.3 percent of children under 12 months of age live in poverty, while only 15.9 percent of children between the ages of 11 to 17 live in poverty (Statistics Canada, 2017a). Children who grow up in a lone-parent home are more likely to suffer poverty, but this dynamic is also gendered, related as it is to the feminization of poverty. Children growing up with a lone mother are twice as likely to be poor as those children who grow up with a lone father (Statistics Canada, 2017a). The Financial Accountability Office of Ontario (2019) published a report noting that lower child-care costs will increase female labour market participation. The report points out that previous studies suggest that every 10 percent decrease in child-care costs would increase the number of women in the workforce by 2 to 4 percent (Financial

Accountability Office of Ontario, 2019). Racialized women experience the intersections of race and gender and are doubly disadvantaged in the workplace. Block et al. (2019) note that racialized women had the highest unemployment rate, at 9.6 percent, while the unemployment rate for non-racialized women was only 6.4 percent. Intersectionality theory complicates the issue of race to explore the complexities of gender discrimination within a patriarchal structure (Crenshaw, 1991).

For immigrants, there exists a wage gap between immigrants with a university degree and Canadian-born persons with the same. Data shows that recent immigrants between the ages of 25 and 54 who hold a university degree earned 70 percent of the wage earned by their Canadian-born university-educated counterparts (Statistics Canada, 2018). Although 70 percent of immigrants arrive in Canada with a post-secondary diploma or degree, their credentials are not always recognized by Canadian employers (Esses et al., 2007). Esses et al. (2007) have argued that immigrants with non-Canadian credentials and experience face "skill discounting." This means that immigrants' foreign-acquired educational and experience-based skills tend to be discounted relative to those of locally trained employees. The effect is that many immigrants end up in lower-status occupations than is otherwise warranted by their education and experience. Additional challenges faced by immigrants include discrimination, language barriers, and lower earnings. Few organizations maintain norms or policies governing the evaluation of foreign credentials. Immigrants may be seen as having a "lack of fit" or as "culturally different" and therefore unsuitable for the position. The field of name-discrimination research provides evidence that non-Anglo-Saxon names are discriminated against in the labour market. Oreopoulos (2011) conducted a Canadian study using 6,000 resumes and found that Anglo-Saxon names received 40 percent more responses from potential employers than "ethnic" sounding names. Bertrand and Mullainathan (2004) examined race in the labour market by sending fictitious resumes to help-wanted ads posted in newspapers in Boston and Chicago. To manipulate perceived race, resumes were randomly assigned African-American- or white-sounding names. White-sounding names received 50 percent more callbacks for interviews, and this racial gap was uniform across occupation, industry, and employer size. This provides evidence of systemic racial discrimination in the labour force. This type of racism results in a labour market that is stratified by race and ethnicity.

The racialization of poverty is another factor linked to socio-economic inequality. The 2016 census indicated that Ontario's overall poverty rate at the time was 14 percent, while for racialized persons that rate was 21 percent. For Black Canadians, the poverty rate was 24 percent (Statistics Canada, 2017b). African-born immigrants had the lowest employment rate and highest unemployment rate of all immigrant groups, and the corresponding differentials with the Canadian-born population were particularly high for African-born newcomers who had been in Canada for five years or less (Statistics Canada, 2018). Block et al. (2019) reported that "racialized workers are more likely to be active in the workforce than non-racialized workers, either working or trying to find work, but this does not result in better employment outcomes for them. From 2006 to 2016, there was little change to the patterns of employment and earnings inequality along racial and gender lines in Canada" (p. 4).

For racialized families living in poverty, financial barriers represent a complex set of interrelated factors that make it difficult to access quality early learning and care. Evans (2004) adopts an **ecological** perspective to illustrate the multiple, cumulative effects of childhood poverty. Many studies focus on the individual and family psychosocial elements and neglect to analyze environmental factors, which are important. According to Evans (2004), poverty exposes children to more violence, crime, family disruption, increased likelihood of out-of-home or foster care, less psychosocial support, less cognitive stimulation, and food insecurity.

Several Canadian studies have found that the implications of low socio-economic status have an effect on school readiness for preschoolers. Cushon et al. (2011) studied the neighbourhood effects of poverty on physical health and well-being in three cohorts of low-income children in Saskatoon, Saskatchewan. They found that physical health and reported emotional well-being declined over time. Wilms (2003) studied risk factors among low-income families in Niagara Falls, Ontario, and found that cognitive and behavioural deficits were higher in children living in lone-parent households, in families with the lowest incomes, and in households where the mother had low levels of education. Janus and Duku (2007), using a teacher-completed Early Development Instrument, determined that children from families with low income score lower on measures of school readiness. Browne et al. (2018) determined that children from economically disadvantaged communities in Canada lag behind their peers in learning outcomes because these families are unable to provide their children with sufficient enrichment during the early years. Kingdon et al. (2017) found significant gender differences among boys and girls identified as "at-risk," with girls attaining higher academic achievement across the years in their longitudinal study. Collectively, the findings from these studies indicate that access to affordable, high-quality early learning and care is essential to overcoming the multiple risk factors associated with low socio-economic status.

There is an abundance of large-scale research evidence from the United States that quality early learning and care benefits low-income children in the areas of **school readiness** (Miller et al., 2016), literacy (Mashburn & Downer, 2013), and socio-emotional behaviour (Jenkins et al., 2018). In Canada, many researchers have also studied the benefits of early learning on low-income children. Pagani et al. (2006) examined whether a preventive enrichment program focusing on pre-math skills for low-income children would enhance numeracy skills. The findings suggested that the pre-math intervention had a positive effect on children's arithmetic learning. Ramirez et al. (2014) studied an intervention program for literacy for children from socio-economically disadvantaged neighbourhoods. The results showed that children improved their vocabulary and morphological skills significantly. Other studies on Indigenous Head Start programs in Canada have determined that the programs provide ample evidence for gains in school readiness (Gerlach & Gignac, 2019; Mashford-Pringle, 2012; Nguyen, 2011).

## Spatial Barriers

**Spatial accessibility** refers to the convenience of physically accessing a service or resource by distance or transportation means (Kim & Wang, 2019). The spatial accessibility of services and resources for low-income families is an environmental challenge that affects children requiring early learning and care. Ferns and Beach (2015) note that the current market-driven approach favouring for-profit early learning centres can result in inequitable access because centres will choose locations likely to be profitable, thereby leaving many without access.

Families living in low-income areas have limited residential mobility and have difficulty accessing affordable housing. They are unable to move to locations with higher-quality early learning or schooling because of their limited incomes (Boschman, 2015). Underserved neighbourhoods have fewer quality resources for health care, food, education, mental health services, and services for persons with disabilities. Low-income neighbourhoods also have fewer parks, green spaces, and local food resources. Low-income neighbourhoods favour high-rise apartment buildings over detached homes. This can create barriers to resources. Homeless families may also lack access to daycare centres or may be forced to use child-care centres at homeless shelters (Hinton & Cassel, 2013).

**Spatial stigma** describes the negative portrayal of low-income areas by the media and in public discourse, with the result that residents experience discrimination simply for living in those areas (Halliday et al., 2020; Pasquetti, 2019). Some geographical areas are highly stigmatized for their high crime rates, low levels of education, high pollution levels, noise, and high unemployment rates. Residents may be reluctant to access services when they must identify their area of residence for fear of stigma (Halliday et al., 2020). Keene and Padilla (2014) also found that spatial stigma contributed to poor mental and physical health.

Many low-income families may be residing in geographical areas with fewer options for high-quality early learning and care. This may lead them to enrol their children in home daycare centres with fewer educational resources or to access child care unregulated altogether.

Low-income families may not have access to a private vehicle and may instead depend on public transit to access child-care centres. This creates additional challenges when it comes to balancing paid work schedules for pickup and drop-off. Citizenship status may also act as a spatial barrier because undocumented persons with children may fear that their attempts to access regulated child-care spaces could lead to deportation. Refugee claimants and asylum seekers may opt for home-based child care within their communities. Refugee parents may also have limited language ability and thus may have reduced access to information about child care and child-care subsidies.

These spatial factors can cumulatively shape the experiences that low-income families have when attempting to access quality early learning and care. Low-income families experience spatial barriers to early learning and care that arise out of their relative socio-economic status. The research indicates that this not only affects the education of their children but also has a long-term impact on health.

## Cultural and Racial Barriers

Despite Ontario's demographic diversity, ECEC curricula and pedagogy in the province has failed to reflect the cultural and racial identities of children and their families. Although early childhood education and care has been discursively constructed as a space of cultural and racial "neutrality," it is epistemologically grounded in Eurocentric, middle-class norms (Butler et al., 2019).

Recent research shows that children become aware of racial differences in infancy and demonstrate same-race preferences for faces (Quinn et al., 2018). The age at which children become aware of race has been the subject of research for decades. Current understandings are that children become aware of race by the age of two or three (De Riggs, 2014; Husband, 2010; McCown, 2004). Children have been known to exclude their peers based on racial categories (Aboud, 2003; Jordan & Hernandez-Reif, 2009). Most problematic is that children begin to show preferences for socially dominant racial identities once they become aware of the significance of race; in the North

American context, that dominant status is held by the Caucasian race (De Riggs, 2014; Newheiser et al., 2014; Pacini-Ketchabaw & Berikoff, 2008). Dulin-Keita et al. (2011) found that racialized children were more aware of race than children from dominant racial groups. Researchers have identified that racial bias in preschool children originates from a combination of parental socialization, peer socialization, and the influence of the popular media (Setoh et al., 2019; Van Ausdale & Feagin, 2001). These research findings suggest that preschool-aged children are aware of race and the social significance of skin colour. The implication for educators is that there is a need to address race and racism in early childhood education curricula and policies.

Unless enrolled in a specialized program such as the Indigenous Head Start program, most Indigenous and racialized children experience early learning curricula that is Eurocentric and does not represent their cultural or racial identities (Derman-Sparks & Edwards, 2019; Escayg, 2019; Vandenbroeck, 2007; York, 2016).

What about the makeup of ECEC professionals? In K–12, the teaching profession tends to be dominated by white, cisgendered, heterosexual, middle-class women. There is a large diversity gap among teachers in Ontario and the Greater Toronto Area (Abawi & Eizadirad, 2020; Turner Consulting Group, 2014). In Ontario, only 10 percent of the province's 70,520 secondary school teachers and 9 percent of its 117,905 elementary school and kindergarten teachers are from racialized groups. In Toronto, racial minorities represent 47 percent of the population yet comprise only 20 percent of secondary school teachers and 18 percent of elementary school and kindergarten teachers (Turner Consulting Group, 2014, para. 9). According to survey data from the Ontario College of Early Childhood Educators, only 1.4 percent of ECEs are male (Ontario Coalition for Better Child Care, 2019, para. 1). Unfortunately, other than data on the number of male-identified ECEs, data regarding the makeup of the ECE profession in Ontario is not readily available, a gap that must be rectified.

What we do know is that white heteronormative biases are manifested in the curriculum, policies, and practices of pre-service ECE programs and early learning settings. In a study of early learning centres, Berman et al. (2017) found that white early childhood educators tended to minimize or ignore racial incidents while also failing to report them. An earlier study by Bernhard et al. (1998) explored the relationships between teachers and families in ethnically diverse ECE settings. The research study of 199 ECE teachers, 77 supervisors, and 108 family members was completed in Toronto, Montreal, and Vancouver. Both teachers and parents reported that racial and discriminatory incidents were not uncommon in child-care centres. Subtle and unintended effects of racism were noticed by some parents more than many teachers. The researchers found that about half (54 percent) of the ECE teachers surveyed observed racial incidents. The majority of teachers took action that included talking to the children (71 percent) while 16 percent did nothing. Only 12 percent chose to involve families in resolving the incidents. From the perspective of the parents, racist incidents were not properly dealt with. Incidents of subtle racism were ignored, and parents of minoritized groups believed that complaining would have negative repercussions for their child. Minimization is one of Bonilla-Silva's (2014) four frames of colour-blind racism. Minimizing or denying racism absolves the individual educator of a responsibility to take action and address racism.

Early childhood education and care in Ontario supports colour-blind racist ideologies (Bonilla-Silva, 2014) through the use of Eurocentric curricula. One of the four frames of colour-blind racism is naturalization, which allows individuals to explain racial phenomena by suggesting that they are natural occurrences. This can be seen when early childhood educators, after witnessing children choose to segregate by race during play, dismiss this as a natural phenomenon instead of a manifestation of covert racism (Aboud, 2003; De Riggs, 2014; Jordan & Hernandez-Reif, 2009).

In summary, low-income racialized families face cultural and racial barriers because of the Eurocentric ECE curriculum and educators' failure to report racist incidents when they occur.

## DISCUSSION

In Ontario, low-income racialized and Indigenous families experience multiple, cumulative barriers that have the effect of reducing or
eliminating their ability to access high-quality early childhood education and care. The quality of early learning matters because it supports
school readiness and healthy development in several domains. The lack
of early support for low-income children puts them at greater risk for
poor academic achievement and poorer psychological well-being. Of
the many life stressors faced by low-income racialized parents, the lack
of adequate child care is one that may impact their ability to secure
employment. For low-income lone-parent families, the importance of
accessible quality early learning is critical.

The many barriers experienced by low-income racialized families
need to be addressed with comprehensive, system-wide supports that
integrate early learning centres with communities, schools, and local
governments. Financial barriers could be eliminated if there was a national system for free public early learning and care. Public investments
in early learning and care should include more child-care spaces, higher
wages for ECEs, and the provision of after-school care. It is evident that
private early learning centres result in disproportionate access based on
higher socio-economic status and neighbourhood factors. Government
interventions should support supply-side funding for early learning that
goes directly to supporting ECEC programs with wages, buildings,
equipment, and resources. Demand-side funding that provides "choice"
to parents benefits mainly middle- and high-income earners who can
enjoy tax breaks.

Combatting racial discrimination in employment would help to ensure that racialized, immigrant, and refugee families are able to provide
safe housing, healthy food, and other resources to support their children. Workplace policies should have strong anti-discrimination and
anti-harassment clauses that hold employers accountable. Equity-and-
inclusion plans for workplaces should include strategies to recruit and
retain qualified applicants from Indigenous and racialized groups.
Public infrastructure spending on affordable public transportation

would reduce barriers for families without vehicles while supporting environmental sustainability.

Racial and cultural barriers also require comprehensive solutions. Early childhood education curricula should adopt an anti-racist education approach (see chapter 9). Escayg et al. (2020) advocate for an anti-racist analysis that is critical of white supremacy and Western knowledge systems. Escayg (2020) proposes a framework for anti-racist early childhood education built on the praxis of anti-oppression and reflective of the epistemologies of racialized and Indigenous groups. The framework adopts a critical perspective on Eurocentric knowledge systems, proposes an anti-racist pedagogy and curriculum, and proposes a reconceptualization of play that recognizes cultural differences. It also presents a counter-narrative to dominant ideologies that treat white supremacy and whiteness as normative (Escayg, 2020). Low-income racialized families would be able to access early learning and care that affirms their children's cultural and racial identities while engaging their parents. These measures would promote the healthy cognitive, emotional, and physical development of racialized and Indigenous children in Ontario.

## CONCLUSION

Without universal access to affordable early childhood education and care, low-income racialized families will continue to face barriers. The research has shown that racialized Ontarians are the most likely to experience racism and discrimination in the labour market. As a consequence, they are more likely to be unemployed or underemployed. The earnings gap between racialized and non-racialized Canadians has persisted over the decades. Systemic changes are required to combat racism in the labour force and in all levels of education. Anti-colonial critical scholars of education Dei and Kempf (2006) remind us that the salience of race is critical to our lived experiences. We must therefore resist the dominant discourse of colour-blind racism and instead advocate for anti-racist and anti-oppressive approaches to early learning curricula

(Bonilla-Silva, 2014). We also need to advocate for more equitable hiring criteria for educators and higher professional wages. It is critical that Ontario moves toward a system of early learning that meets the needs of low-income racialized children and families. A more inclusive system of early learning and care would benefit all Ontarians.

## CRITICAL THINKING QUESTIONS

1. Describe some of the specific barriers facing low-income racialized families when it comes to accessing high-quality child care.
2. In what ways is an intersectional approach necessary for exploring the experiences of low-income racialized families?
3. How is colour-blind racism reinforced in early childhood education settings?

## GLOSSARY OF KEY TERMS

**colour-blind racism:** A term created by Bonilla-Silva (2014) to describe a racist ideology that claims not to see racial differences while simultaneously discriminating against others based on racial categories.

**ecological:** A term used to describe the relationship between an individual and their environment.

**intersectionality:** A term created by legal scholar Kimberlé Crenshaw (1991) to describe how social identities such as race, gender, class, and sexuality are connected to form unique social experiences.

**LICO (Low-Income Cut Off):** Statistics Canada (2015) defines a LICO as an "income threshold ... below which a family will likely devote a larger share of its income on the necessities of food, shelter and clothing than the average family" ("What are the LICOs?" section).

**low income:** Income levels that are at or just above poverty level, with little disposable income.

**racialized:** Since "race" is a social construct, this term is used to describe the societal process by which some individuals are "raced" based on phenotypical traits such as skin colour (Omi & Winant, 2015).

**school readiness:** There are many context-specific definitions of school readiness, but the term generally refers to a young child's readiness for school based on domains that include cognitive, socio-emotional, and physical.

**spatial accessibility:** The convenience of physically accessing a service or resource by distance or by means of transportation (Kim & Wang, 2019).

**spatial stigma:** The ways that low-income and racialized neighbourhoods are adversely represented in the media and in policy-making and public discourses.

## REFERENCES

Abawi, Z., & Eizadirad, A. (2020). Bias-free or biased hiring? Racialized teachers' perspectives on educational hiring practices in Ontario. *Canadian Journal of Educational Administration and Policy, 193*, 18–31.

Aboud, F. E. (2003). The formation of in-group favoritism and out-group prejudice in young children: Are they distinct attitudes? *Developmental Psychology, 39*(1), 48–60.

Association of Early Childhood Educators Ontario. (2017). *Transforming work in Ontario's early years and child care sector: Workforce strategy recommendations presented to the Ministry of Education, November 30, 2017.* https://www.aeceo.ca/transforming_work_in_ontario_s_early_years_and_child_care_sector

Berman, R., Daniel, B., Butler, A., McNevin, M., & Royer, N. (2017). Nothing or almost nothing to report: Early childhood educators and discursive constructions of colorblindness. *International Critical Childhood Policy Studies Journal, 6*(1), 52–65.

Bernhard, J., Lefevbre, M., Kilbride, K., Chud, G., & Lange, R. (1998). Troubled relationships in ECE: Parent-teacher interactions in ethno culturally diverse child care settings. *Early Education and Development, 9*(1), 5–28.

Bertrand, M., & Mullainathan, S. (2004). Are Emily and Greg more employable than Lakisha and Jamal? A field experiment on labor market discrimination. *American Economic Review, 94*(4), 991–1013.

Block, S., Galabuzi, G., & Tranjan, R. (2019). *Canada's colour coded income inequality.* Canadian Centre for Policy Alternatives.

Bonilla-Silva, E. (2014). *Racism without racists: Color-blind racism and the persistence of racial inequality in the United States*. Rowan & Littlefield.

Boschman, S. (2015). Selective mobility, segregation and neighbourhood effects. *A+BE: Architecture and the Built Environment, 11*, 1–190.

Browne, D. T., Wade, M., Prime, H., & Jenkins, J. M. (2018). School readiness amongst urban Canadian families: Risk profiles and family mediation. *Journal of Educational Psychology, 110*(1), 133–146.

Butler, A., Teasley Severino, C., & Sánchez Blanco, C. (2019). A decolonial approach to disrupting whiteness, neoliberalism, and capitalist pedagogy in Western early childhood education and care (ECEC). In P. Trifonas (Ed.), *Handbook of theory and research in cultural studies and education* (pp. 1–18). Springer International.

Child Care Advocacy Association of Canada. (n.d.). *Child care in Canada by 2020: A vision and a way forward*. Retrieved January 21, 2021, from http://childcare2020.ca/sites/default/files/VisionChildCare2020Nov3ENG_.pdf

Collins, P. H. (2000). *Black feminist thought: Knowledge, consciousness, and the politics of empowerment*. Routledge.

Crenshaw, K. W. (1991). Mapping the margins: Intersectionality, identity politics, and violence against women of color. *Stanford Law Review, 43*(6), 1241–1299.

Cushon, J. A., Vu, L. T. H., Janzen, B. L., & Muhajarine, N. (2011). Neighborhood poverty impacts on children's physical health and well-being over time: Evidence from the early development instrument. *Early Education and Development, 22*(2), 183–205.

Dei, G. J. S., & Kempf, A. (2006). *Anti-colonialism and education: The politics of resistance*. Sense Publishers.

De Riggs, V. (2014). *A study of the origins of racial awareness in preschool aged children*. ProQuest Dissertations.

Derman-Sparks, L., & Edwards, J. (2019). Understanding anti-bias education: Bringing the four core goals to every facet of your curriculum. *YC Young Children, 74*(5), 6–12.

Dulin-Keita, A., Hannon I. L., Fernandez, J., & Cockerham, W. (2011). The defining moment: Children's conceptualization of race and experiences with racial discrimination. *Ethnic and Racial Studies, 34*(4), 662–682.

Escayg, K.-A. (2019). "Who's got the power?" A critical examination of the anti-bias curriculum. *International Journal of Child Care and Education Policy, 13*(1), 1–18.

Escayg, K.-A. (2020). Antiracism in U.S. early childhood education: Foundational principles. *Sociology Compass*, *14*(4), 1–15.

Esses, V. M., Dietz, J., Bennett-Abuayyash, C., & Joshi, C. (2007, Spring). Prejudice in the workplace: The role of bias against visible minorities in the devaluation of immigrants' foreign-acquired qualifications and credentials. *Canadian Issues*, 114–118.

Evans, G. W. (2004). The environment of childhood poverty. *American Psychologist*, *59*(2), 77–92.

Ferns, C., & Beach, J. (2015). From childcare market to childcare system. *Our Schools, Our Selves*, *24*(4), 43–62.

Financial Accountability Office of Ontario. (2019). Child care in Ontario: A review of Ontario's new Child Care Tax Credit and implication for Ontario's labour force. https://www.fao-on.org/en/Blog/Publications/childcare-ontario-2019

Friendly, M. (2015). Taking Canada's child care pulse: The state of ECEC in 2015. *Our Schools, Our Selves*, *24*(4), 7–24.

Friendly, M., & Prentice, S. (2009). *About Canada: Childcare*. Fernwood.

Gerlach, A. J., & Gignac, J. (2019). Exploring continuities between family engagement and well-being in Aboriginal Head Start programs in Canada: A qualitative inquiry. *Infants & Young Children*, *32*(1), 60–74.

Halfon, S., & Langford, R. (2015). Developing and supporting a high quality child care workforce in Canada: What are the barriers to change? *Our Schools, Our Selves*, *24*(4), 131–143.

Halliday, E., Popay, J., de Cuevas, R. A., & Wheeler, P. (2020). The elephant in the room? Why spatial stigma does not receive the public health attention it deserves. *Journal of Public Health*, *42*(1), 38–43.

Hinton, S., & Cassel, D. (2013). Exploring the lived experiences of homeless families with young children. *Early Childhood Education Journal*, *41*(6), 457–463.

Husband, T. (2010). He's too young to learn about that stuff: Antiracist pedagogy and early childhood social studies. *Social Studies Research and Practice*, *5*(2), 61–75.

Husband, T. (2012). "I don't see color": Challenging assumptions about discussing race with young children. *Early Childhood Education Journal*, *39*, 365–371.

Janus, M., & Duku, E. (2007). The school entry gap: Socioeconomic, family, and health factors associated with children's school readiness to learn. *Early Education and Development*, *18*(3), 375–403.

Jenkins, J. M., Sabol, T. J., & Farkas, G. (2018). Double down or switch it up: Should low-income children stay in Head Start for 2 years or switch programs? *Evaluation Review, 42*(3), 283–317.

Jordan, P., & Hernandez-Reif, M. (2009). Re-examination of young children's racial attitudes and skin tone preferences. *Journal of Black Psychology, 35*(3), 388–403.

Keene, D. E., & Padilla, M. B. (2014). Spatial stigma and health inequality. *Critical Public Health, 24*(4), 392–404.

Kim, H., & Wang, F. (2019). Disparity in spatial access to public daycare and kindergarten across GIS-constructed regions in Seoul, South Korea. *Sustainability, 11*(19), 5503.

Kingdon, D., Serbin, L. A., & Stack, D. M. (2017). Understanding the gender gap in school performance among low-income children: A developmental trajectory analysis. *International Journal of Behavioral Development, 41*(2), 265–274.

Martinez-Lopez, M. (2020, August 29). Protestors across Canada march to defund the police. *CTV News.* https://www.ctvnews.ca/canada/protesters-across-canada-march-to-defund-the-police-1.5084956

Mashburn, A. J., & Downer, J. T. (2013). Methods that examine the extent to which the quality of children's experiences in elementary school moderate the long-term impacts of Head Start. *Society for Research on Educational Effectiveness*, 1–6. https://files.eric.ed.gov/fulltext/ED563295.pdf

Mashford-Pringle, A. (2012). Early learning for Aboriginal children: Past, present and future and an exploration of the Aboriginal Head Start Urban and Northern Communities Program in Ontario. *First Peoples Child & Family Review, 7*(1), 127–140.

McCown, C. (2004). Age and ethnic variation in children's thinking about the nature of racism. *Journal of Applied Developmental Psychology, 25*(5), 597–617.

Miller, E. B., Farkas, G., & Duncan, G. J. (2016). Does Head Start differentially benefit children with risks targeted by the program's service model? *Early Childhood Research Quarterly, 34*, 1–12.

Morgan, H. (2010). Young white children see race. *Race, Gender and Class, 17*(1), 114–117.

Newheiser, A., Dunham, Y., Merrill, A., Hoosain, L., & Olson, K. (2014). Preference for high status predicts implicit outgroup bias among children from low-status groups. *Developmental Psychology, 50*(4), 1081–1090.

Nguyen, M. (2011). Closing the education gap: A case for Aboriginal early childhood education in Canada, a look at the Aboriginal Head Start program. *Canadian Journal of Education, 34*(3), 229–248.

Office of the Premier. (2018, April 26). More than 3,100 new child care spaces for families across Ontario: Province creating new spaces ahead of implementing free preschool child care [Press release]. https://news.ontario.ca/opo/en/2018/04/more-than-3100-new-child-care-spaces-for-families-across-ontario.html

Omi, M., & Winant, H. (2015). *Racial formation in the United States.* Routledge.

Ontario Coalition for Better Child Care. (2019). Around 1 percent of early childhood educators are men. https://www.childcareontario.org/around_1_percent_of_early_childhood_educators_are_men

Oreopoulos, P. (2011). Why do skilled immigrants struggle in the labor market? A field experiment with thirteen thousand resumes. *American Economic Journal. Economic Policy, 3*(4), 148–171.

Pacini-Ketchabaw, V., & Berikoff, A. (2008). The politics of difference and diversity: From young children's violence to creative power expressions. *Contemporary Issues in Early Childhood, 9*(3), 256–264.

Pagani, L. S., Jalbert, J., Lapointe, P., & Hébert, M. (2006). Effects of junior kindergarten on emerging literacy in children from low-income and linguistic-minority families. *Early Childhood Education Journal, 33*(4), 209–215.

Pasquetti, S. (2019). Experiences of urban militarism: Spatial stigma, ruins and everyday life. *International Journal of Urban and Regional Research, 43*(5), 848–869.

Quinn, P., Lee, K., & Pascalis, O. (2018). Perception of face race by infants: Five developmental changes. *Child Development Perspectives, 12*(3), 204–209.

Ramirez, G., Walton, P., & Roberts, W. (2014). Morphological awareness and vocabulary development among kindergarteners with different ability levels. *Journal of Learning Disabilities, 47*(1), 54–64.

Setoh, P., Lee, K., Zhang, L., Qian, M., Quinn, P., Heyman, G., & Lee, K. (2019). Racial categorization predicts implicit racial bias in preschool children. *Child Development, 90*(1), 162–179.

Shah, T. I., Bell, S., & Wilson, K. (2016). Spatial accessibility to health care services: Identifying under-serviced neighbourhoods in Canadian urban areas. *PloS One, 11*(12). https://doi.org/10.1371/journal.pone.0168208

Statistics Canada. (n.d.). *Statistics on Indigenous Peoples.* Retrieved January 21, 2021, from https://www.statcan.gc.ca/eng/subjects-start/indigenous_peoples

Statistics Canada. (2015, November 27). *Low income cut-offs.* https://www150.statcan.gc.ca/n1/pub/75f0002m/2012002/lico-sfr-eng.htm

Statistics Canada. (2017a, September 13). *Children living in low-income households*. https://www12.statcan.gc.ca/census-recensement/2016/as-sa/98-200-x/2016012/98-200-x2016012-eng.cfm

Statistics Canada. (2017b, October 25). *Ethnic and cultural origins of Canadians: Portrait of a rich heritage*. http://www12.statcan.gc.ca/census-recensement/2016/as-sa/98-200-x/2016016/98-200-x2016016-eng.cfm

Statistics Canada. (2018, December 24). *The Canadian immigrant labour market: Recent trends from 2006 to 2017*. https://www150.statcan.gc.ca/n1/pub/71-606-x/71-606-x2018001-eng.htm

Turner Consulting Group. (2014, October 30). *Teacher diversity gap*. https://www.turnerconsultinggroup.ca/blog-tana-turner/teacher-diversity-gap

Van Ausdale, D., & Feagin, J. (2001). *The first R: How children learn race and racism*. Rowman & Littlefield.

Vandenbroeck, M. (2007). Beyond anti-bias education: Changing conceptions of diversity and equity in European early childhood education. *European Early Childhood Education Research Journal, 15*(1), 21–35.

White, L. A., Perlman, M., Davidson, A., & Rayment, E. (2019). Risk perception, regulation, and unlicensed child care: Lessons from Ontario, Canada. *Journal of Risk Research, 22*(7), 878–896.

Wilms, D. (2003). *Early childhood development in Niagara Falls, Ontario: Understanding the early years*. Human Resources and Skills Development Canada, Service Canada.

York, S. (2016). *Roots and wings: Affirming culture and preventing bias in early childhood* (3rd ed.). Redleaf Press.

CHAPTER 3

# Troubling Dominant Discourses and Stories that Shape Our Understanding of the Child Refugee

*Nidhi Menon*

## LEARNING OBJECTIVES

- To discuss and consider how certain stories can become dominant and be understood as the truth even though they only present one point of view
- To understand agency and vulnerability in the lives of refugee children
- To identify the damage inflicted by dominant deficit discourse on the lives of refugee children
- To explore ways of rethinking damage-centred research
- To engage with a pedagogy of discomfort as a process for revisiting early childhood educators' pedagogy and practice

Truth is not always opposed to power: truth can help produce knowledge, experts, and a "discipline," to legitimize hegemonic practices. (Chimni, 2009, p. 18)

## INTRODUCTION

In this chapter I intend to present the importance of the stories we tell and listen to, and how through these stories we understand ourselves and our relationships and make meaning of the world in which we live. I question the stories that we come to understand as universal. These stories, in their telling and retelling, situate themselves as the truth, influence our beliefs and decisions, and become absolute truths that we do not think to question. This chapter, which looks at Canada's commitment to resettle over 40,000 Syrian refugees fleeing their country's civil war, is an attempt to question the stories about young refugee children in our early childhood settings (IRCC, n.d.). Although refugees from many different places call Canada their home, this chapter focuses specifically on the plight of Syrian refugees due to Canada's widespread resettlement initiative.

Our absorption in our personal struggles, especially our COVID-19 realities, must be viewed in relation to the wider world in crisis, in which children and families continue to be displaced by war, natural disasters, and a myriad of other factors. In this reality, early childhood educators' relationships with refugee children in early childhood settings are shaped by the stories that emerge as dominant discourses influencing pedagogies and exerting a great influence on the way we think and behave. Foucault refers to this as "a regime of truth" (as cited in Moss, 2019, p. 5), directing what we see as the truth and influencing power relationships. This chapter questions the subjective perspectives that assert themselves as the only reality, which in turn skews our understanding of the lived experiences of refugee children.

Representations of refugee children in public discourse often invoke images of poverty, homelessness, mental and physical anguish, and sometimes even death. These public discourses are fuelled by research about refugees that is entrenched in debates over mental health, lack of resources, skills, rights, and the need for protection (Hassan et al., 2015; Sirin & Rogers-Sirin, 2015). This reflects what Tuck (2009) refers to as **"damage-centred research"** (p. 412). These discourses portray the deficits of child refugees in a way that seems to take hold of our senses and our thoughts, and, consequentially, they construct a dominant narrative of child refugees as a "lost generation," "weak," "vulnerable," and "in need" (Sirin & Rogers-Sirin, 2015). There is no question that war and displacement have contributed to these children's vulnerability and victimization to a certain degree, but does that mean that becoming a refugee has stripped them of their **agency**? Why do we, in our zeal to protect these young children, look at them as objects to be pitied? Why is our gaze arrested on their deficits and not on their strength and resiliency?

In a bid to critically think about the lived experiences of Syrian refugee children in early childhood settings, I present critical thinking as a two-pronged approach. The first involves a process of recognizing, enquiring, and challenging dominant views of refugee children that we understand as the absolute truth. The second involves constituting, proposing, and discovering alternatives to demonstrate that there are additional ways to understand a concept. So, critical thinking in this chapter represents both a *de*construction and *re*construction. It also represents a commitment to troubling the dominant deficit framework affiliated with the discourse surrounding refugee children, and to presenting alternate viewpoints.

This chapter is composed of two sections. The first presents the research that has contributed to the dominant images of refugee children as "vulnerable," "suffering," "at risk," and "in need." I situate this **dominant deficit discourse** within the framework of **developmentalism**, which is fuelled by the normative ideal of the "neoliberal child" who is constantly viewed as an incomplete adult in the making (Gabriel, 2014; Moss, 2019; Woodhead & Faulkner, 2008). In the second section, I present an argument that troubles the "normative" definitions of agency and vulnerability and rethink dichotomies that pit vulnerability against agency (Butler, 2016; Klocker, 2007; Sutterlüty & Tisdall, 2019). This allows us to understand the lives of refugee children beyond objectivity, developmentalism, and universal theories. I present lessons that emerge from the intersections of **decolonial studies, post-structural feminism**, and the **"new" sociology of childhood** with the goal of transforming pedagogy and practice in early childhood education.

## SITUATING REFUGEE CHILDREN WITHIN THE PARADIGM OF DEVELOPMENTALISM

Of the 6.3 million global refugees since 2011 (UNHCR, n.d.), Canada has received more than 40,000 Syrian refugees, a group composed mostly of families with young children. According to Statistics Canada (2019), 44 percent of these Syrian refugees were under the age of 15. Even though there has been an active interest in studying Syrian refugees, the population actively researched is predominantly youth and adults. The experiences of young children are mostly subsumed by researchers within the family unit, with the result that these children are rarely treated as individuals in their own right or members of a specific social group.

Through the narratives of youth and adult family members, we understand that children fleeing the war in Syria continue to experience stressful life events, such as the death of a family member or being in a dangerous situation, and these have contributed to their precarious life experiences. Multiple studies, several of which were conducted in refugee camps, show that Syrian refugee children experience a lower quality

### Box 3.1

"Syria is the biggest humanitarian and refugee crisis of our time, a continuing cause of suffering for millions which should be garnering a groundswell of support around the world" (UN High Commissioner for Refugees Filippo Grandi, as cited in UNHCR, 2016). The war in Syria has displaced more than 6.6 million refugees since 2011 (UNHCR, 2016). In 2015 and 2017, Syrian refugees outside of Syria made up the largest population of displaced refugees in the world, and by the end of 2017, nearly 1 in 10 of the world's refugees were from Syria (UNHCR, n.d.). Approximately 40 percent of the Syrian refugees are under 12 years of age. Canada was one of the key destinations for many Syrians taking refuge from the country's civil war (UNHCR, n.d.).

of life, anxiety, post-traumatic stress disorder, depression, and psycho-somatic problems, among other difficulties (Sirin & Rogers-Sirin, 2015). These studies pay particular attention to the vulnerability of these children, and they raise the alarm about the "prospect of a 'lost' generation" if the "mental health needs of vulnerable refugee children are left unaddressed," which will "negatively impact their successful development into adulthood" (Sirin & Rogers-Sirin, 2015, p. 14).

The studies that focus on the traumatic experiences and vulnerability of Syrian refugee children and youth have played a crucial part in informing the organizations and individuals caring for them, not to mention the wider world, about the suffering experienced by this population, including the problems they face and their many unmet needs. While there is no question that these studies are important, there is a need to trouble the underlying discourse of the "lost," "weak," "constantly suffering," and "vulnerable" child, and to supplement this discourse with alternative strength-based frameworks and narratives. We need to be aware that studies that portray refugee children as suffering, vulnerable, and forgotten are steeped in deficit frameworks that maintain a discourse in which the refugee child is portrayed as a failure—someone who is damaged and incomplete, and at times even subhuman.

To challenge the notion of a "lost generation," we need to understand the deeper, implicit message that this kind of research conveys: that refugee children are passive, non-agentic innocents who are acted upon by the world (Gabriel, 2014). The literature about refugee children and youth portrays the refugee experience as a "universality," which serves to maintain developmental psychology's view of children and child development as linear, a view underpinned by an evaluative Euro-centric framework that dismisses the multiplicity of childhoods along with children's agency (Burman, 2008). These studies problematize child refugees' identities and growth in relation to normative Eurocentric processes of socialization (Gabriel, 2014). With the disruption of the key influences in the child's micro and macro systems—such as the family, educators, and schools—there is an urgency for them to learn "the 'laid-down' patterns of values that will mould them into existing society"—in other words, to be "properly" socialized (Gabriel, 2014, p. 119).

Additionally, studies that focus on trauma and its impacts on refugee children successfully highlight the impact of organized violence and forced displacement on their mental health while mapping their atypical development in the physical, cognitive, social, and emotional domains. Put differently, these narratives treat refugee children as deficient.

These findings regarding "faulty" socialization and the impact of trauma result in "discourses about ages and stages [that] become linked to developmental norms, encoded in milestones and developmental delay" (Gabriel, 2014, p. 120). While using this framework to view children, childhood is conceptualized as an "apprenticeship for adulthood" (p. 120), with the consequence that refugee children are portrayed as vulnerable and deficient. As Gabriel (2014) notes, "young children are viewed as a set of 'potentials,' 'a project in the making,' researched within an evaluative framework that is mainly interested in their position on the stage-like journey to mature, rational, responsible, autonomous, adult competence" (p. 121).

Critiquing the dominant developmental psychology lens, Woodhead and Faulkner (2008) emphasize that it is not surprising that the child is treated as an object of dispassionate observation, one to be studied and characterized by child development experts and psychologists to produce a rhetoric of refugee childhood experiences as universal. The individuality of refugee children and their experiences are detached and reduced to a set of measures that can be counted, sorted, and categorized to fit a certain set of behaviours (Gormez et al., 2018; Hands et al., 2015; Hoot, 2011). Researchers within the developmental psychology paradigm treat children as people in the making, which Verhellen (1997) describes as "a state of 'not yet being'" (p. 15). This creates and maintains the dominant image of the refugee child as a "'human becoming' rather than a 'human being'" (Woodhead & Faulkner, 2008, p. 15).

Scholars of childhood have worked tirelessly to uncover the lived experiences of children and to assert that children are individuals who have a present and future, thus troubling the dichotomy of "being" versus "becoming" (Uprichard, 2008). Hanson (2017) problematizes this dichotomy by reminding us that children not only have a present and a future but also a past, which we seem to be forgetting. In the case of child refugees, the urgency to submit to the dominant discourse of "lost childhoods" not only has us view these children as unable to follow the normative path to become competent adults, it also strips them of their agency in their present lives while completely deleting their past. To transcend the being/becoming dichotomy, we need to situate the refugee child historically and politically in time as an agentic social actor in their own right, one who is actively constructing their own childhood and who has views and experiences about being a child.

At an international level, the **United Nations Convention on the Rights of the Child (UNCRC)** (1989) has been and continues to be a major impetus for reforming existing policy and reimagining a protectionist framework for the "vulnerable" child. Providing protection, early intervention, and prevention have been major areas of study and change, as has emphasizing an individualist ideology that treats children as the principal stakeholders in their own lives who are capable of exercising their rights and advocating for their needs. Even though the UNCRC encouraged researchers to "listen" to children's voices, understand their thoughts and beliefs, and respect their experiences and ideas, a critical and deeper analysis of this work uncovers the hidden agenda of some researchers who wish to covertly maintain the hegemony of the adult/child, competent/incompetent dualisms. According to Woodhead and Faulkner (2008), this research continues to focus on "cognitive or memory processes, stages of relative competence, normality, deviation and pathology" (p. 13). Even though this is not true of all research conducted about and on children (see MacNevin & Berman, 2016), there is nonetheless a large body of research about refugee children and youth that uses UNCRC frameworks that produce "data" that is heavily dependent on an adult interpretation of child development. This adult-centric lens produces and disseminates information that is often couched in a discourse of child welfare promoting the need for quality in care and education (Woodhead & Faulkner, 2008). While it may seem counter-intuitive, using a rights-based discourse to study children is tantamount to using a deficit discourse rooted in a binary framework: that of the vulnerable victim who is lacking and the benevolent state that provides a form of protection that is mirrored by research, policy, and practice.

We need to wonder how dominant discourses like that of the broken refugee child achieve their positions of dominance. Why do we believe them to be the ultimate truth? According to Moss (2019), an insidiousness underlies the dominant discourse of the weak, non-agentic vulnerable refugee child rooted in a "management and control" (p. 15) narrative of **neoliberalism**. The core concepts of standardization, accountability, linearity, individualism, and universality that neoliberalism perpetuates and maintains have permeated our pedagogy and practice, creating mechanisms for oppression, marginalization, and exclusion. Judging refugee children through a developmentalist framework only serves to focus on their deficits, and thereby socializes them into neoliberal and capitalist norms of success (Moss et al., 2016; Simpson et al., 2015). This ideological underpinning is the hidden agenda of the patriarchal state, which seeks to continue dominating the bodies of these children. So how does the dominant discourse about refugee children affect them? Does the pervasiveness of the dominant deficit discourse make them believe and accept this discourse as their reality? If so, what are the consequences for these children?

## THE DANGERS OF DOMINANT DEFICIT DISCOURSE AND DAMAGE-CENTRED RESEARCH

Trauma-informed research offers us an in-depth view of human suffering. But the images, attitudes, and knowledge it invokes become the dominant lens through which refugees are viewed, and this takes a powerful hold in our minds and hearts and dominates our senses. Even though this kind of research is an essential part of recognizing the suffering of refugees, there is nonetheless a need to trouble the dominant discourse of refugee children as a "lost generation" because we need to understand the "long-term repercussions of thinking ourselves as broken" (Tuck, 2009 p. 409). Freire (1973), adopting a **praxis of equity and social justice**, urged us to recognize our inhumanity when we fail to recognize an "unjust order that engenders violence in the oppressors, which in turn dehumanizes the oppressed" (p. 26).

To understand the real impact of damage-centred research driven by the developmental paradigm, we turn to Indigenous scholar Eve Tuck (2009), who cautions us that understanding individuals as a sum of their deficits situates not just them but entire communities as worthy of alienation and rejection. Our pity maintains and sustains structural inequalities in these communities, which "become spaces saturated in the fantasies of outsiders" (Tuck, 2009, p. 412). Tuck (2009) argues that if we were to critically deconstruct the agenda behind stories that centre deficit, we would find that these stories of damage are encapsulated in discourses of support, protection, resiliency, and care. Similarly, hooks (1990) claims that, to "only speak from that space in the margin that is a sign of deprivation, a wound, an unfulfilled longing" (as cited in Tuck, 2009, p. 413), dehumanizes these children, which consequentially reduces them merely to their pain and deficits.

When we hear, believe, and accept damage-centred images without questioning them, we blind ourselves to their "hidden cost" (hooks, 1990). At this juncture, we must question our ethics and the politics that have led us to adopt these beliefs. Even though our intentions may be good, we must think about the outcomes of adopting deficit thinking as praxis when learning along with refugee children, and how even with good intentions we can be complicit in enacting harm. Tuck (2009) urges us to adopt a reflexive approach and to ask critical questions about whom this information will benefit and the human cost that results from pedagogies rooted in these kinds of research.

Bringing our understanding of damage-centred research to bear on the historical exploitation and maltreatment of the land and resources of Indigenous Peoples through colonization and domination, Tuck (2009) argues that the multitude of research on the suffering of a certain population has the ironic effect of making them invisible. Looking at refugee displacement, there is an abundance of research on young refugee children and how their displacement has negatively influenced their lives. And yet a closer inspection reveals that most of these narratives emerge from family members or older children (13 years and older). The more refugee stories we read, the harder it is to locate the perspectives of younger children. This is what damage-centred research does: it cleverly and deliberately withholds and makes invisible the harm resulting from the intersection of capitalism, neoliberalism, patriarchy, racism, and colonization. As a consequence, our gaze becomes fixed on the damage. We continue to be colonized by research that does not acknowledge the wider context of colonization and the resulting damage to our bodies, families, and communities.

Indigenous communities, communities of colour, and refugees once welcomed this kind of research because it was accompanied by an unwritten message that their participation would provide a way out of their present situation, that it would help change the narrative of oppression and domination and bring about social change and justice. But did it? Instead, what we see happening is an urgency to police these children and their identities; under the guise of protectionism, we evaluate them against Western and Eurocentric norms of development and deem them "at risk," "vulnerable," and a "lost generation."

To trouble the dominant deficit discourse, Tuck (2009) suggests an epistemological shift by adopting a "researching for desire" framework (p. 409). This is not about substituting one form of thinking for another; instead, it is about the desire to think carefully and generously of the vulnerabilities and needs of research participants, knowing that there may be multiple ways of understanding these concepts. We need to be aware of historical and current contexts while maintaining a willingness to unearth hidden narratives—narratives that take account of "complexities, contradiction, and the self-determination of lived lives" (Tuck, 2009, p. 416). In the context of child refugees' lived experiences, this awareness provides a framework through which to understand their vulnerability, agency, and ultimately their humanity.

## A Pedagogical Shift in Our Thinking: Re-Imagining Agency

### Box 3.2

Shames, as cited in Wolfe (2019) was displaced from Syria along with her mother when she was nine. She is a child. She is also the lone provider of her family. As she told one interviewer, "I always worry about my mother's health, but not mine. I can manage. But I want her to be safe and healthy" (as cited in Wolfe, 2019). Just like Shames, there are millions of child refugees who work, provide for their families, and act as caregivers, support systems, and decision makers for the adults in their lives. Shames and children like her constantly have their agency evaluated by researchers, policy-makers, and educators against a "normative" framework, and many are seen as "negative," "wanting," "abnormal," and "ambiguous."

Why are we quick to criticize, raise alarm, and marshal reinforcements to normalize the agency of refugee children, which we think makes them "weak," "vulnerable," "at risk," and "in need"?

The concept of young children exercising agency has been and continues to be a key area of interest in the new sociology of childhood. Sutterlüty and Tisdall (2019) argue that this deeply entrenched tendency in both political and research agendas is fuelled by researchers from a variety of disciplines and by policy-makers and bureaucrats who advocate for children's rights. If agency is a celebration of children's competency, why is refugee children's agency treated as something we need to remedy? It is also worth asking: What is agency, and how can it be explained in the context of refugee children? Why is it essential to gain an understanding of this concept so that we can understand refugee children's lived experiences? According to Mayall (2002), agency in children refers to their ability to negotiate with others, which creates agency in regards "to a relationship or to a decision, to the workings of a set of social assumptions or constraints" (p. 21).

Through multiple ethnographic studies exploring the life experiences of children, the concept of agency started to be viewed through a positive lens that provided children a voice. Even though this conceptualization of agency seems to serve the dominant political and research agenda, it also helped create a normative framework against which all forms of agency were evaluated. It was also defined as something that children possessed innately and could act upon according to their own free will, which ignored the influence of relationships and power dynamics in children's lives (Sutterlüty & Tisdall, 2019).

Gallagher (2019) critiques the normative concept of agency by arguing that research about agency and voice in childhood studies, which is supposedly designed to empower children to make their voices heard, may contain within it a hidden agenda related to policing and the imposition of normative forms of agency regulating how children should behave. As a result, individuals who do not fit the dominant neoliberal mould are often excluded. Refugee children, by the very nature of where they have been and what they have experienced, exercise agency despite and through their vulnerabilities (Gallagher, 2019).

To trouble these explanations, Sutterlüty and Tisdall (2019) question where children's "ambiguous agency" or agency that goes against the social norm fits. In the context of child refugees, it is essential to disrupt these norms because refugees' lives are synonymous with atypical and unpredictable lived experiences. Agency in the lives of refugee children will need to be reframed through a relational lens and within the context of their experiences. Refugee children, depending on their particular situations and contexts, and their relationships with other people and institutions, may experience agency in myriad ways.

Some scholars (see Klocker, 2007; Tanyas, 2012) have theorized that agency in children may be placed on a continuum ranging from thick to thin, "which varies depending on opportunistic and constrained contexts, created and expected identities, positions of powerlessness, life-course stages and state of emotions and wellbeing" (Tisdall & Punch, 2012, p. 255). Following Klocker (2007), Sutterlüty and Tisdall (2019) argue that "a celebration of children's agency can ignore how some children are highly circumscribed by their contexts or other circumstances, failing to perceive how children's agency is 'thinned' by such aspects rather than 'thickened'" (p. 184). These children can be viewed as vulnerable and lacking agency in certain contexts and exerting agency in others. In spite of, and even in the midst of, extreme circumstances, they can experience thickness of agency when they influence many local situations, such as when they create strong supportive social relationships in heterogeneous assemblages that include people, things, and organizations (Archambault, 2012; Betancourt & Khan, 2008; Gallagher, 2019; Tanyas, 2012).

## Rethinking Vulnerability

To be recognized as and labelled a refugee, and to avail oneself of the protection this label entails, individuals must be constructed as vulnerable and lacking agency. According to Bhabha (2007), who has undertaken extensive study of the displacement of children from a legal perspective, children who transcend international boundaries "become non-citizens or aliens once they cross a border" (p. 1); additionally, children are perceived as "family dependents who lack autonomous agency" (p. 2). Bhabha (2007) also shows that, legally, "for purposes of immigration law, a 'child' only exists in relation to a parent" (p. 2). To cross borders and apply for asylum or refugee status, families are required to prove parent-child relationships and produce an assurance of the child's dependency on the parents. So, the refugee and legal system, including border control, is designed around adults, and particularly in relation to parents. The dominant discourse of the vulnerable refugee child exists in relation to the agentic child. But what if we view refugee children's vulnerabilities as their strength? Could we understand vulnerability as more than its dominant normative definition as a deficit?

Butler (2016), a post-structural feminist scholar, thinks it is essential to view agency as a type of opposition to vulnerability. Adopting a feminist praxis, Butler (2016) gives us an opportunity to rethink and refocus our gaze and to embrace the realization that weakness alone does not present a complete understanding of vulnerability. She urges us to ask: What if we relinquish a binary mode of thinking, stop pitting agency against vulnerability, and instead start viewing them alongside each other? Espousing this praxis permits us to understand the connections between vulnerability, agency, and individualism. Using a feminist critique allows us to understand the true nature of ontologies of injustice and inequalities that maintain and sustain the oppression and violence inflicted upon all minorities by dominant ways of thinking. It disrupts our skewed understandings of vulnerability as a merely subjective embodiment by troubling its connections to individualism, which is deeply embedded in hegemonic, masculinist, and Western neoliberal epistemologies that disqualify what women, children, and minorities deem essential for equality and freedom.

Butler (2016) challenges us to view vulnerability beyond an opposition to agency in order to rethink it as a "deliberate exposure to power" (p. 22), as a conscious decision to be involved and to stay involved. In this sense, vulnerability is agency, resistance, mobilization, and above all a political act.

Refugee children use vulnerability to dismantle and disrupt paternalism and its power, thereby establishing themselves as agentic resistors and political beings capable of disrupting the hegemonic discourse. Within and among relationships, children are open to change; they can feel, think, and thrive while also placing themselves at risk (Gallagher, 2019). The intensity of the relationship between children's vulnerabilities and their capacities for action is key to our deeper understanding of these concepts. In many relationships, when their agency might be thinned, children still find a way to exert agency "despite or against the dominant orientations of the power relations within an assemblage" (Gallagher, 2019, p. 193).

Butler (2016) emphatically states that "vulnerability is not a subjective disposition" (p. 25). Researchers working with children against this dominant backdrop urge us to trouble this discourse by engaging with the relational aspect of knowledge production. Thinking within the framework of relational sociology, Farmer and Cepin (2017) argue that researchers can serve as facilitators who can co-create a climate of inquiry, learning, curiosity, and wonder. Educators practise reflexivity while reflecting along with children. This space opens opportunities for children to be vulnerable and dependent on others while exercising their agency to create change in their world. It also values the fact that children are in relationships with adults and their peers, navigating spaces, negotiating meaning, and transforming ideas and environments. This draws attention to the learning happening within the assemblage of educators, children, and non-human entities that constitute teaching and learning. We can understand the lives and lived experiences of refugee children by foregrounding the knowledge that we are in this world together: occupying different social locations but learning about a world we share together and striving to understand each other.

## Reconsidering Discomfort

Education is a political practice, and when educators adopt certain pedagogical positions, they make a political statement. Paulo Freire (1973) encouraged educators to critically reflect on their pedagogies in an effort to continually challenge, modify, and dismantle current power structures that maintain hegemonies and oppression. To answer Freire's call is to critically rethink our pedagogies, complicate our practice, make ourselves vulnerable to an uncomfortable process, and become aware of the politics of our pedagogy and practice. It is a call to trouble our prior understandings and to recognize that we may be complicit in the production and reproduction of dominant discourses. This process is complicated, to say the least. It will also require us to experience acute discomfort.

Boler (1999) helps us adopt a praxis of equity by inviting us to think with a "pedagogy of discomfort" (p. 176). One of her many calls within this pedagogical stance includes thinking critically with the popular pedagogical reflective practice. One of the tenets of a pedagogy of discomfort is to question "cherished beliefs and assumptions," because this process is "an invitation to inquiry as well as a call to action" (Boler, 1999, p. 176). To accomplish this, educators need to shake off their complacency and adopt an ethics that questions their attachment to their preconceived notions.

Boler (1999) asks us to step into the pedagogy of discomfort by troubling the process of self-reflection that is often touted as an invaluable practice by educators. She questions this process and urges us to recognize its deep roots in Western individualism. What we adopt ethically and willingly as a process of pedagogical inquiry may in reality "reduce genuine inquiry to an individualized process with no collective accountability" (Boler, 1999, p. 177). To immerse oneself in discomfort, one needs to go beyond the individualized process of self-reflection and step into the threshold and realm of "collective witnessing" (Boler, 1999, p. 176). This is a deliberate strategy aimed at leaving behind the comforting, liberal process to which self-reflection is often reduced; instead, we must step into the vulnerabilities that emerge in a collective process, in which we may feel exposed, scrutinized, and threatened. This process can cause certain emotions to rise to the surface—including "defensive anger, fear of change, and fears of losing our personal and cultural identities" (Boler, 1999, p. 176). This pedagogical orientation urges us to recognize how our emotions "define how and what we choose to see, and conversely, not to see" (Boler, 1999, p. 176); how our beliefs, actions, and emotions have become stagnant, impervious, and rigid; and how we seem to ignore the untold stories and certain "truths" that have been created in opposition to certain omissions and silences. How can early childhood educators change narratives and bring about equitable change by adopting a pedagogy of discomfort? Practising "collective witnessing" within relationships with refugee children, families, colleagues, communities, and others, early childhood educators can place themselves in discomfort, and step willingly into a space of vulnerability that has potential for transformation. What kinds of narratives might emerge from this space in which refugee children tell their stories from their own perspectives? How might these stories transform our pedagogies, practice, and view of refugee children? The hope is that by adopting this pedagogical orientation, we can create a pedagogy of resistance that troubles the dominant deficit discourse to create social transformation and address inequities.

## CONCLUSION

In this chapter, I have attempted to explain the deficit perspectives underlying the dominant discourse of refugee children. I conclude by revisiting Chimni's (2009) assertion that truth is powerful: it can produce knowledge, but it can also uphold hierarchies and maintain hegemonies while asserting itself as the ultimate reality. By examining motivations of researchers who stand to gain from work that sustains a deficit perspective, hidden agendas—in this case, the desire to maintain neoliberal ideologies of "us" and "them"—are explored. Ideas for how early childhood educators can work with young refugee children in a manner that goes against the dominant deficit discourse were discussed; specifically, I called for the adoption of a pedagogy of discomfort in order to problematize narratives of the suffering, troubled refugee child and the universality of the refugee experience. Understanding refugee children requires a process of acknowledging the complexity, fluidity, and mobility of childhoods. By engaging in this process, we can move closer to languages of hybridity and non-linearity and enter a framework of relationality. We must respect the vulnerabilities and lived realities of children as they come to understand themselves in and among the dynamic relationships that define their subjectivities and what it is to be a child who is also a refugee. Informed by decolonial studies, post-structural feminism, and the "new" sociology of childhood, I have set out ways of rethinking, re-imagining, and reconsidering the supposed deficits of refugee children so as to appreciate them and embrace an "ontology of immaturity" (Gallacher & Gallagher, 2008, p. 511), and to accept ourselves as always changing, evolving, incomplete, immature, and vulnerable. I urge early childhood educators to welcome the strengths and potentials of these complex qualities. In doing so, we can provide a positive space for learning—a space in which we can share with others and gain the courage to tell stories from various viewpoints.

## CRITICAL THINKING QUESTIONS

1.  What is your understanding of deficit discourse? How does this discourse become dominant in our communities?

2.  How does developmentalism contribute to a deficit discourse or damage-centred narrative?

3.  How can you understand agency in the context of the lived experiences of refugee children? Why is their agency considered ambiguous?

4. Using Butler's (2016) description of vulnerability as a strength rather than a weakness, describe a time where you used vulnerability to overcome a challenging personal circumstance?

5. How can you adopt a pedagogy of discomfort as a method of inquiry and action to confront personal biases and belief systems?

## GLOSSARY OF KEY TERMS

**agency:** The ability of children to negotiate with others, which creates an impact on their relationships, decisions, and on society's expectations of them.

**damage-centred research:** Indigenous scholar Eve Tuck (2009) describes this as research centred on the damage sustained by certain communities, which results in their being described as defective.

**decolonial studies:** An area of study that proposes that the power imbalances created by colonization did not end with colonialism, but instead continue to reverberate long after the political rule of the colonizer is abolished.

**developmentalism:** The application of a Eurocentric, Western view of children and childhood as unilinear, predictable, and eternal, and which posits the existence of a supposedly normal or typical development and trajectory.

**dominant deficit discourse:** Socially organized frameworks of meaning that are dominant or popular in research policy and public life, and that affect our general way of being in and construction of the world. By contrast, a discourse of deviation from what is considered typical or the norm is seen as negative and as a disadvantage.

**neoliberalism:** A concept that has infiltrated all aspects of our lives valuing competition, standardization, accountability, linearity, individualism, and universality, and which in turn perpetuates and maintains mechanisms for oppression, marginalization, and exclusion.

**"new" sociology of childhood:** A paradigm that views childhood as a social construct and children as competent social actors who are capable of making decisions and affecting the relationships they have with others, rather than as passive subjects affected by top-down socialization.

**post-structural feminism:** An area of feminist studies that makes visible such binaries as child/adult and normal/abnormal through an analysis of texts and talk in order to understand how relations of power, especially as they connect to gender, are constructed and maintained.

**praxis of equity and social justice:** The process by which issues of disadvantage, discrimination, and inequity are applied, exercised, or enacted.

**United Nations Convention on the Rights of the Child (UNCRC):** The most complete statement of children's rights and the most widely ratified human rights treaty in the world. Its 54 articles address all facets of a child's life to make sure the rights of all children are secured.

## REFERENCES

Archambault, J. (2012). It can be good there too: Home and continuity in refugee children's narratives of settlement. *Geographies, 10*(1), 35–48.

Betancourt, T. S., & Kahn, K. T. (2008). The mental health of children affected by armed conflict: Protective processes and pathways to resilience. *International Review of Psychiatry, 20*(3), 317–328.

Bhabha, J. (2007). *Independent children, inconsistent adults: International child migration and the legal framework.* UNICEF Innocenti Research Centre, Innocenti Discussion Papers.

Boler, M. (1999). *Feeling power: Emotions and education.* Routledge.

Burman, E. (2008). *Deconstructing developmental psychology.* Routledge.

Butler, J. (2016). Rethinking vulnerability and resistance. In J. Butler, Z. Gambetti, & L. Sabsay (Eds.), *Vulnerability in resistance* (pp. 12–27). Duke University Press.

Chimni, B. S. (2009). The birth of a "discipline": From refugee to forced migration studies. *Journal of Refugee Studies, 22*(1), 11–29.

Farmer, D., & Cepin, J. (2017). Researching along with children and youth: Using creative visual methods throughout the research process. In T. Skelton (dir.) &

R. Evans (co. dir.), *Geographies of children and young people: Vol 2. Methodological approaches* (pp. 303–333). Springer.

Freire, P. (1973). *Pedagogy of the oppressed.* Seabury Press.

Gabriel, N. (2014). Growing up beside you: A relational sociology of early childhood. *History of the Human Sciences, 27*(3), 116–135.

Gallacher, L. A., & Gallagher, M. (2008). Methodological immaturity in childhood research? Thinking through "participatory methods." *Childhood, 15,* 499–516.

Gallagher, M. (2019). Rethinking children's agency: Power, assemblages, freedom and materiality. *Global Studies of Childhood, 9*(3), 188–199.

Gormez, V., Kılıç, H. N., Orengul, A. C., Demir, M. N., Demirlikan, Ş., Demirbaş, S., Babacan, B., Kinik, K., & Semerci, B. (2018). Psychopathology and associated risk factors among forcibly displaced Syrian children and adolescents. *Journal of Immigrant and Minority Health, 20*(3), 529–535.

Hands, C., Thomas, J., & John-Legere, S. (2015). Refugee children in the UK. *Paediatrics and Child Health, 26*(1), 37–41.

Hanson, K. (2017). Embracing the past: "Been," "being" and "becoming" children. *Childhood, 24,* 281–285.

Hassan, G., Kirmayer, L. J., Mekki-Berrada, A., Quosh, C., el Chammay, R., Deville-Stoetzel, J. B., Youssef, A., Jefee-Bahloul, H., Barkeel-Oteo, A., Coutts, A., Song, S., & Ventevogel, P. (2015). *Culture, context and the mental health and psychosocial wellbeing of Syrians: A review for mental health and psychosocial support staff working with Syrians affected by armed conflict.* UNHCR. http://www.unhcr.org/55f6b90f9.pdf

hooks, b. (1990). *Yearning.* South End Press.

Hoot, J. L. (2011). Working with very young refugee children in our schools: Implications for the world's teachers. *Procedia Social and Behavioural Sciences, 15,* 1751–1755.

IRCC [Immigration, Refugees and Citizenship Canada]. (n.d.). *#WelcomeRefugees: Key figures.* Retrieved May 1, 2020, from https://www.canada.ca/en/ immigration-refugees-citizenship/ services/refugees/welcome-syrian-refugees/ key-figures.html

Klocker, N. (2007). An example of thin agency: Child domestic workers in Tanzania. In R. Panelli, S. Punch, & E. Robson (Eds.), *Global perspectives on rural childhood and youth: Young rural lives* (pp. 81–148). Routledge.

MacNevin, M., & Berman, R. (2016). The Black baby doll doesn't fit: The disconnect between early childhood diversity policy, early childhood educator practice, and children's play. *Early Child Development and Care, 187*(5–6), 827–839.

Mayall, B. (2002). *Towards a sociology of childhood: Thinking from children's lives.* Open University Press.

Moss, P. (2019). *Alternative narratives in early childhood.* Routledge.

Moss, P., Dahlberg, G., Grieshaber, S., Mantovani, S., May, H., Pence, A., Rayna, S., Swadener, B. B., & Vandenbroeck, M. (2016). The Organisation for Economic Co-operation and Development's International Early Learning Study: Opening for debate and contestation. *Contemporary Issues in Early Childhood, 17*, 343–351. https://doi.org/10.1177%2F1463949116661126

Simpson, D., Lumsden, E., & McDowall Clark, R. (2015). Neoliberalism, global poverty policy and early childhood education and care: A critique of local uptake in England. *Early Years: An International Research Journal, 35*, 96–109. doi:10.1080/09575146.2014.969199

Sirin, S., & Rogers-Sirin, L. (2015). *The educational and mental health needs of Syrian refugees.* Migration Policy Institute. http://www.migrationpolicy.org/research/educational-and-mental-health-needs-syrian-refugee-children

Statistics Canada. (2019, February 12). *Syrian refugees who resettled in Canada in 2015 and 2016.* https://www150.statcan.gc.ca/n1/daily-quotidien/190212/dq190212a-eng.htm

Sutterlüty, F., & Tisdall, E. K. M. (2019). Agency, autonomy and self-determination: Questioning key concepts of childhood studies. *Global Studies of Childhood, 9*(3) 183–187.

Tanyas, B. (2012). Making sense of migration: Young Turks' experiences in the United Kingdom. *Journal of Youth Studies, 15*(6), 693–710.

Tisdall, E. K. M., & Punch, S. (2012). Not so "new"? Looking critically at childhood studies. *Children's Geographies, 10*(3), 249–264.

Tuck, E. (2009). Suspending damage: A letter to communities. *Harvard Educational Review, 79*(3), 409–428.

UNHCR [United Nations High Commissioner for Refugees]. (n.d.). *Syria emergency.* Retrieved January 21, 2021, from https://www.unhcr.org/syria-emergency.html

UNHCR. (2016, March 15). Syria conflict at 5 years: The biggest refugee and displacement crisis of our time demands a huge surge in solidarity [Press release]. https://www.unhcr.org/news/press/2016/3/56e6e3249/syria-conflict-5-years-biggest-refugee-displacement-crisis-time-demands.html

United Nations. (1989). Convention on the Rights of the Child. *Treaty Series, 1577,* 3.

Uprichard, E. (2008). Children as "being and becomings": Children, childhood and temporality. *Children & Society, 22*(4), 303–313.

Verhellen, E. (1997). *Convention on the Rights of the Child.* Garant.

Wolfe, D. (2019). *Refugee: Shames' story.* World Vision. https://www.worldvision.ca/stories/refugees/refugee-shames-story

Woodhead, M., & Faulkner, D. (2008). Subject, objects or participants. In P. Christensen & A. James (Eds.), *Research with children: Perspectives and practices* (2nd ed., pp. 10–39). Routledge.

CHAPTER 4

# Equity Enacted: Possibilities for Difference in ECEC through a Critical Ethics of Care Approach

*Alana Powell, Lisa Johnston, and Rachel Langford*

## LEARNING OBJECTIVES

- To discuss and describe key themes and critiques in an ethics of care
- To question and think critically about your understanding of equity
- To describe how equity is framed in ethics of care
- To reconsider equity in practice through an ethics of care framework
- To reflect critically on the possibilities for professional preparation programs to enact equity through an ethics of care framework

## INTRODUCTION

Equity, based on the notion of equal rights, is increasingly present in policies, procedures, and dialogues relating to early childhood education and care (ECEC) in Ontario. Yet equity has yet to be "realized" in practice. Inequitable access to ECEC services and poor working conditions for predominantly female educators is the reality; there is also a lack of equity within ECEC services, with some children, families, and educators continuing to face exclusion and marginalization. We continue to see the lack of equity in educational practice predominantly impacting

Indigenous people, individuals living with disabilities, and racialized groups across the province (Shewchuk & Cooper, 2018). We believe the understanding of equity as equal rights does not go far enough. Instead, we suggest it is necessary to shift our conceptual understanding of what equity is. We draw upon an **ethics of care** (Hamington, 2018; Langford et al., 2017; Robinson, 2019; Tronto, 2013) to suggest a conceptual move that thinks of equity as something **enacted**, or put into action, in relation with others in early childhood settings.

The ethics of care puts caring responses that are emotionally attuned to the particular situations of others at the centre of ethical decision making. The ethics of care emerged in response to traditional moral theory, which insists on detached, logical ethical decision making, thereby setting the mind over the body, the self over others, and male over female. These **master binaries** create ideas of what is normal and abnormal in our society, and in so doing position "difference" as a problem in social relations. What exists outside the norm becomes different, lesser-than, devalued, undesirable, and unworthy. In response to this, care scholars, inspired by the primary work of Carol Gilligan (1982, 2011), assert another way of thinking about ethics and moral theory—one that brings forth the importance of interdependency, emotions, and the particular situations of others. Robinson (2019) and other care scholars maintain that, at its core, the ethics of care recognizes difference and includes diverse ways of caring about and for others. Moreover, the priority of contextual sensitivity in the ethics of care means that discursive practices in ethical decision making always work against the tendency to put people and things into binaries and categories that marginalize and exclude some voices. The ethics of care thus creates space for seeing how everybody and everything is in relation to and dependent on someone and something else.

We begin this chapter by considering the ethics of care as moral theory and practice that provides an opportunity to think about how equity is enacted in relations with others in the moment. We examine how, as a critical **post-foundational theory**, the ethics of care is attuned to context, to difference, and to the relational, thereby creating possibilities for invention (Robinson, 2019). Drawing on Tronto (1993, 2013), we consider the phases of care as a way to understand equity enacted in relations with others, as well as how our institutions may establish the conditions within which this experimentation can occur. We also consider professional preparation programs for educators an important site for disruption and transformation, where we can interrupt the current narrow conceptualization of equity in favour of other methods of bringing equity to life in meaningful ways. Finally, we consider how thinking **equity in relations** and within a critical ethics of care opens up possibilities at the philosophical, political, and practice levels.

## THE ETHICS OF CARE AS RESISTANCE TO TRADITIONAL MORAL THEORY

Right from its inception, the ethics of care has been concerned with equity. Gilligan (1982) questioned the influential research of Lawrence Kohlberg (1981), who claimed that girls' moral development is deficient because they seek solutions to ethical decision making through caring for others, empathy, and sensitivity to contextual details rather than through objective, abstract principles in which the same response applies to all persons—in other words, an ethics of universal justice. In her research on girls' moral development, Gilligan (1982, 2011) found a new way of thinking about responses to ethical decision making, which she called an ethics of care.

Gilligan's work on care ethics has garnered three key criticisms concerned broadly with equity. First, critics argued that the ethics of care, with its initial focus on girls and women, essentializes care by treating it as a feminine trait, and thereby potentially reinforces values such as female selflessness and self-sacrifice, which work against feminist equity goals. Second, the ethics of care has been perceived as a private, personal ethics—not one concerned with "public," political, or social justice issues. The third critique suggests that the ethics of care prioritizes gender and does not consider other human differences.

Many critics initially challenged Gilligan's work for its focus on the experience of girls and women, which from these critics' perspective, reinforces care as a feminine trait. However, care ethicists argue that an ethics of care is only a "feminine practice" under patriarchal conditions, in which women and racialized groups are expected to do invisible and devalued care work. Gilligan (2011) considers an ethics of care to be a human ethic accessible to all of humanity when it is released from its subordinate position in **patriarchy**. Thus, when we talk about educators as carers, we are always thinking about how caring is a human practice.

Related to this first criticism are concerns that favouring an ethics of care, with its claim that persons are interdependent and unequal under systems of oppression, leads to the rejection of an ethics of justice, which claims that persons are autonomous and have equal rights. However, most ethics of care scholars argue for "some kind of complementary relationship between care and justice ethics" (Hankivsky, 2014, p. 254). For example, the right of all persons to flourish and secure their well-being motivates them to care ethically for others (Hamington, 2004). Still, most care scholars consider care, rather than the notion of universal justice, more fundamental to human life because, as Held (2006) states, the survival of our world depends on care. Furthermore, Held (2006) maintains that care has always been performed by women and racialized groups, who assume a disproportionate responsibility for it. Importantly, we suggest that caring well for each other and advancing the conditions upon which care occurs represent important moves toward a more just and equitable world.

A second criticism centres on what is thought to be a narrow focus in the ethics of care on the personal and private world of the family. This criticism has spurred a broadening of care ethics into the realm of political theory and social justice (Engster & Hamington, 2015). For example, Held (2006) offered a philosophical account of care ethics as a distinct moral theory that "addresses rather than neglects moral issues arising in relations among the unequal and dependent" at the personal, political, and global levels (p. 13). Further, Joan Tronto (2013) offered a political examination of how care thinking and practices are confined to the invisible, devalued private realm of the family. Fisher and Tronto (1990) broadened the definition of care to focus on "the maintenance, continuation and repair of our 'world' so that we can live in it as well as possible" (p. 40). Tronto's (2011) analysis and application of care into four phases (and later five; see Tronto, 2013) informs later sections of this chapter. Tronto (2013) also sets out a political analysis of how women and racialized groups in democratic societies assume respons-ibility for the care of others, while certain privileged groups use various justifications (e.g., men can get out of caring because they "bring home the paycheque") to escape from care responsibilities.

Tronto (2013) also explores tensions between ethics of care scholars over the best place (whether at the interpersonal or political level) to address power imbalances in care relations. Some scholars suggest that enacting compassion and recognition of vulnerability and suffering in interpersonal care relations provides "a basis for counterbalancing in-equalities in care" (van Heijst & Leget, 2011, p. 8). In contrast, Tronto (2011) argues that inequalities in care relations are addressed when care is made a central value in democratic societies. According to Tronto (2011), underpinning this central value are three ideas: that all human beings need care; that democratic work is needed to ensure equality of care responsibilities; and that care is better when it is done democrat-ically or collectively (pp. 45–47). In this chapter, we focus on the inter-personal, social, *and* political levels.

A third criticism of the ethics of care concerns what some scholars perceive as its narrow focus on gender to the exclusion of race, class, and other social categories. Contemporary issues of globalization, mass migration, hyper-capitalism, and environmental crisis have heightened this criticism. Second- and third-generation scholars, building on the political considerations of care, have therefore centred their work on ex-ploring how gender, race, ethnicity, class, sexuality, nationality, and dis-ability intersect with power and privilege in care relations. For example, Olena Hankivsky (2014), a political scientist, explores intersectionality as an important theoretical and critical resource for the development of care ethics:

> Intersectionality explicitly rejects the prioritization of hierarch-
> ical orderings of any social category such as gender even when at-
> tempts are made to attend to individuals and groups in holistic and

context-specific ways. In attending to the more complex context of human lives, intersectionality also transcends additive (race + gender + class) or multiplicative analyses (race × gender × class) and instead focuses on the meaning and consequences of interactive and interlocking social locations, power structures, and processes. (p. 253)

Hankivsky uses the case of migrant care work to show how care ethics, in dialogue with the theory of intersectionality ("intersectionality-inspired care ethics"), yields complex understandings of diversity and power relations. In Canada, one example of migrant care workers is nannies from the **global South** who care for young children in their employers' homes. A variety of factors, including country of origin, gender, ethnicity, religion, and immigration status, affect power imbalances in these nanny-employer relationships and the level of remuneration given to the nannies. Nevertheless, we regard gender as an important social factor for both nannies and early childhood educators because they are predominantly women. As Altman and Pannell (2012, p. 292) state, "gender matters but it does not always matter in the same way, and it is not the only factor that matters: class, race and nationality are equally salient" (as cited in Hankivsky, 2014, p. 257).

Similarly, Nalinie Mooten (2015) seeks to link ethics of care with Gayatri Spivak's (1998) **post-colonial theory** to develop a post-colonial ethics of care with three key premises. The first highlights the potential for **paternalism** in relationships in which, for example, an educator is white and the children and families they care for are non-white newcomers to Canada. The second premise then insists in such a situation on an orientation of humility, introspection, attentiveness, and on listening so as to counter paternalism in relationships. The third premise argues for an awareness of how colonialism is also reworked in this situation, such that migrant care workers such as nannies from formerly colonized countries in the global South are expected to be thankful for any kind of work in the **global North**, even that undertaken in inhumane working conditions.

While acknowledging the value of the concept of intersectionality for understanding care work, Robinson (2019) argues that there is an inherent resistance in the ethics of care to "all binaries [such as men and women and 'us and them'] that divide people into categories and separate them from others, and, indeed from themselves" (p. 11). Drawing extensively on Gilligan (2011), Robinson suggests that criticisms of "only gender in analyses of care" and "Western-centrism" arise when it is assumed that care work is synonymous with care as an ethic (p. 10). For Robinson (2019), while differences across time and place are evident in care work, care as a critical ethical and political theory locates "difference at the very core" of care relations (p. 14). Therefore, Robinson (2019) writes, "care ethics has the potential to contest racial and **neo-colonial hierarchies**" and to allow "for the possibility that care is practised in different ways in different places" (p. 16). Following Robinson (2019), we see care as an ethic enacted relationally in early childhood settings as a way of living and being with others that resists binaries and hierarchies. In terms of practice, we find the concept of intersectionality helpful when it comes to thinking about "differing expectations and/or experiences within and across social categories" (Hankivsky, 2014, p. 256). As Robinson (2019) suggests, thinking with difference allows us to think contextually and simultaneously about power, privilege, and identity. It requires us to think with intersectionality when making decisions and judgements about how we care. This is essential to how we see equity as a possibility when enacted in caring relations with others.

## WHY (RE)THINK EQUITY AS EMBODIED

When thinking about opportunities for creating equity and equitable outcomes, we often consider equity at a macro level or as an abstract concept; this is the case, for example, with child-care centres whose policies describe commitments to the inclusion of children with disabilities. We acknowledge that equity in these places is important. We believe that these places and the documents that govern them shape our understanding of equity and create the conditions through which equity can be enacted, enlivened, and brought to life. But we suggest that equity at the abstract, macro level, as described above, is not enough.

What, then, does equity look like if we cannot define it or describe it abstractly? How will we know it exists? When we look to an abstract definition of equity, it contains several key features. Unlike equality, equity does not mean that we all receive the same treatment—in fact, it includes an explicit recognition that we do not all have the same opportunity and we should not be treated in the same "fair" way. As such, equity as a concept is about the process by which we create experiences that, given the context, provide a more just experience—in which, perhaps, the potential outcome becomes fairer. To think critically about current notions of equity, review box 4.1.

What is necessary for an educator to determine if a scenario is equitable is an understanding of what could be in place for children to be able to participate; this must include the perspectives and feelings of the children, as well as a critical recognition of the histories and context of all involved. Therefore, we find that thinking about equity in abstract, broad terms may be useful for developing policy frameworks—but in practice, we must think of equity as something experienced, lived, and understood in relations with others.

This is not to suggest that educators must abandon efforts to address inequity on socio-political and structural levels. We consider

## Box 4.1

In a preschool classroom, three children want to use scissors to cut paper. If an educator decides there should be only one pair of scissors, no equality exists for the children to engage in cutting paper. You add two more pairs of scissors, and now we can claim that equality exists—each child has the same opportunity to participate in cutting paper. But is it equitable? Can we discern this without an understanding of the children in the program, the complexities, nuances, and histories of the place? Perhaps one child is left-handed and struggles to use the right-handed scissors. Perhaps one child cannot stand to reach the table, or they have never used scissors before. You cannot abstractly observe this scenario and determine that it is equitable. You must know the specific context.

these efforts necessary and important. However, when it comes to understanding equity, we must consider an important alternative, one that is situational, contextual, and messy, and made visible in relations with others. We will look to Hamington (2018) to think about care and equity as **embodied** or as something that is tangible and visible, and we will consider how equity may come to life using Tronto's (1993) four phases of care. We will then consider what the process of care lends to an educator's understanding of equity in practice with young children. Finally, we will consider Tronto's (2013) fifth phase of care as we explore possibilities for shifting our understanding of equity at the macro level.

Hamington (2018) states that "care is not merely about establishing a moral disposition or a structure for adjudicating ethical dilemmas, but is fundamentally experiential in requiring action on behalf of others" (p. 310). This suggests, importantly, that care cannot only be understood as a way to think about our moral actions, but instead must be understood by an educator as an act that occurs as an embodied experience. What is important in this idea is that if care is embodied, then in order for an educator's care to occur, they must accord the utmost importance to how a child, family member, or colleague experiences care. Hamington (2018) continues: "The person in need is the final arbiter of responsive care. Their needs and growth determine the efficacy of care; therefore, not every act done in the name of care (e.g. corporal punishment or colonial paternalism) constitutes care as defined within care ethics" (p. 311). We suggest here that equity must be understood in this same way—not as something that exists only as a disposition or structure, but as something that is lived, experienced, and embodied by both the givers and receivers of care. Hamington (2018) makes this claim by illuminating examples of care delivered in a way that is not caring, like colonial paternalism. In Canada in the nineteenth and twentieth centuries, the colonization of Indigenous populations was erroneously considered at that time to be "in their best interests." However, had the perspectives and experiences of Indigenous people been considered, then one would determine (as many of us have in recent years) that these actions were violent, harmful, unjust, and deeply uncaring.

In thinking about early childhood, an early years educator may have a robust policy that establishes a commitment to equity and outlines ways to "achieve equity," yet if children, families, and educators do not *feel* equity, if they do not *experience* equity, we must say that equity as ethical care does not exist. So how do we think about understanding and determining whether equity has been experienced?

## PHASES OF CARE AS EQUITY ENACTED

Care is an ongoing and relational process. Tronto (1993) considers four phases for the exploration of care processes: *caring about*, *taking care of*, *caregiving*, and *care receiving*, to which she later (2013) adds a fifth, *caring with*. The first phase, *caring about*, is where the educator as a caregiver recognizes there is an unmet need for care. The educator here makes a judgement that there is a need for care based on their relationship with the care receiver and the context they are in. In the second phase, the educator must take responsibility for the care need—Tronto (1993) calls this *taking care of*. Here, the educator decides that they will respond to the need for care. This takes thoughtful consideration from the caregiver and a recognition of who the care receiver is, including the power relations, nuances, and histories of the context they come from and currently occupy. The third phase of care, *caregiving*, is when the care is delivered. The educator has made a judgement about the best way to deliver this care and the caring act occurs. This judgement is based on the previous knowledge considered in the caring relationship, and care is delivered in a way that respects both the giver and receiver of care. It is important here that care does not add to power imbalances and inequities, but rather acts to disrupt and challenge them.

In the fourth phase, *care receiving*, the receiver of care (child, family member, educator) acknowledges whether care has been delivered in a way that has met their needs. This is an important phase, as it recognizes the notion that the care receiver must be respected and heard as part of the care process. If implemented successfully, this phase provides an opportunity to demonstrate, in action, that the caregiver should not be privileged over and or hold power over the care receiver—in fact, the care receiver must hold space in the care relation. Tronto (2013) added a fifth phase, *caring with*, which will be explored later in this chapter. These phases of care involve mutual respect, responsiveness, and responsibility, and they seek to disrupt power imbalances between the giver and receiver of care in a way that reflects the place, space, time, and context of the encounter.

Let us now turn to thinking with the phases of care as a process for enacting equity in early childhood. The first phase, caring about, opens an opportunity for us to recognize an unmet need. In this context of equity, this allows us to address hierarchy (education is more important than care), binary (typical or atypical development), or injustice (a child is excluded on the basis of a disability). These, of course, are determined in relations with others and in the reflection of the place, space, and time of these relations. For example, we can consider the following questions: In this moment, what structures and histories establish unjust conditions? What characteristics, contextual nuances, and power relations contribute to this context? And, What differences, binaries, and hierarchies exist that create an inequity? In practice with young children, much of this will be understood by the caregiver. An early childhood educator must commit to knowing the histories and contexts of the space, place, and time in which they operate, and the differences/binaries/hierarchies/power relations that are embedded in their relationships. This will shape and inform how an educator responds to inequity in a matter of moments throughout their day.

The educator must then decide to meet the care need, or, in this case, address the inequity. This must be done with thoughtful consideration of all the aforementioned elements that complexify the context and relation. A caring act can then occur, meaning an act can be taken to address the identified inequity. Here the educator makes a judgement based on the messy and complex context and relationships in which an ethical, meaningful, and disruptive act is required. This act must be disruptive to the hierarchies, binaries, structures, or conditions that create, amplify, and entrench inequities. Then, as in care receiving, the experiences of the care receiver must be acknowledged. Was their need met?

Do they *feel* that inequity has been addressed? Are they able to engage in a way previously closed to them because of the inequity? If the care receiver acknowledges that inequity was addressed, we can then consider equity experienced. Now, does this mean that inequities no longer exist, or that the care receiver has had all barriers removed? It does not. These moments happen in multiple ways throughout a day; they help to disrupt the inequities experienced and create a more liveable world. This is a move toward a more equitable world. In thinking with care ethics and equity, we can see how these concepts allow us to be attuned and responsive to the context, messiness, and intersectionality of identities, as well as to specific circumstances and opportunities, as opposed to merely applying an abstract understanding of what equity is or how it is to be achieved in practice.

What we are not suggesting here is that there is only one right way to care, or one right way to address inequities in practice. Instead, we suggest that in thinking with the elements of the ethics of care (interdependency, responsibility, attentiveness, contextual sensitivity), we can think differently about our role in enacting equity in practice—thereby ensuring that equity is experienced and embodied. In thinking with the phases of care, we suggest not a structured, linear process for enacting equity, but a way to think about bringing equity to life in relations with others in a way that deeply values their experience and voice while actively disrupting inequitable structures and conditions. If, then, the goal is to move toward thinking of equity as enacted, we must now discuss what we consider as necessary at the social and political levels in order for the early years sector to get there—a process that involves *caring with*.

## CARING WITH: OPPORTUNITIES TO RE(THINK) EQUITY

*Caring with* extends the phases of care into the political and the public, considering care as essential to the goals of democracy. Tronto (2013) asserts that "caring needs and the ways in which they are met need to be consistent with democratic commitments to justice, equality and freedom for all" (p. 23), acknowledging that we are all equal in our interdependence on one another as receivers of care but that care needs vary among individuals and groups and at different times. Arguing for care as a political theory, Tronto (2013) recognizes that if we are to achieve a caring democracy, the public conception of care needs to change. For a society to be truly democratic, to move beyond merely thinking of democracy in terms of voting and elections, Tronto (2013) identifies the need for governments to assign responsibilities for caring while also ensuring that citizens have a say in how these responsibilities are assigned. This is not the case in Ontario, for example, where the early childhood education and care sector is left to the mercy of the private market. This perpetuates the private-public divide and the illusion that child care is apolitical, even though much of this work is done in public, non-profit centres. Considering educational institutions as political tools that shape us as future citizens and reinforce dominant narratives in society—such as how we think about and value those who engage in care work—we see these sites as critical for changing public conceptions of care, especially among educators themselves. We argue that early childhood education (ECE) professional preparation programs in Ontario, which uphold traditional moral theories and colonial interpretations of care, need to examine and disrupt these dominant narratives in favour of an understanding of equity as an embodied experience enacted in caring relations.

The roots of the inequities faced by early childhood educators in practice can be traced to professional preparation programs in Ontario colleges and universities and to the glaringly apparent lack of a critical discourse of care and equity. Traditional moral theories, embedded in developmentalism, continue to create binaries and hierarchies (Robinson, 2019), which is evident in the preference for education over care (Langford et al., 2017). Indeed, foundational child development theories that make up the syllabi of ECE programs silently reinforce the importance of educating the minds of young children over caring for their bodies and minds. Consider also that care is not taught in college classrooms but by early childhood professionals in field practicum settings. How does this delineation also sustain the hierarchies organizing those that teach the mind and those that care for bodies? Are we not then teaching aspiring educators to devalue their own work and to place the value of education over care? ECE students graduate every year carrying the mantle of the expert in child development, which is then invoked to legitimize their work as more than "just wiping noses and changing diapers." Furthermore, educators are also subject to gendered hierarchies through the cherished narrative of child-centred pedagogy. Langford (2010) argues that this hierarchy places children, specifically male children, at the centre of early childhood relationships, which renders educators invisible as they are then considered a "facilitator" or system component, as opposed to an important subject or being in the relationship. In child-centred pedagogies, educators become hidden in the background (Langford, 2010) in the same way, according to Tronto (2013), that care is often hidden, or "backgrounded," behind neoliberal economic discourses about workers and economic growth. These discourses are embedded in ECE's hidden curriculum aimed at educating children as future citizens who can function successfully in a neoliberal society.

Traditional moral theories in ECE professional preparation programs are also located within the good educator/bad educator binary. As ECE students are introduced to the Code of Ethics and Standards of Practice established by the College of Early Childhood Educators in Ontario in 2007, conversations about professional ethics, which may arguably be the only conversation about ethics found within ECE programs, are now front and centre and, we argue, very problematic. Drawing on Tronto's (2013) discussion of personal responsibility in a caring democracy, the presence of a regulatory body for the ECE profession in Ontario gives the government a pass when it comes to taking responsibility for the problems faced by the workforce (e.g., low wages and poor working conditions). These problems are caused by the location of ECE programs in the private market-driven system, which directly and indirectly impact educators' ability to provide good care and education. As previously discussed, educators take responsibility for the Other, but they do not have the conditions in place to do this in a way that is not harmful to them or that allows the necessary time to engage in the caring relations that lead to equity. Instead, all responsibility for a broken child-care system and "bad" care is downloaded through the regulatory body onto individual educators. While Tronto (2013) does not deny that personal responsibility is necessary, she does argue that it cannot be the only form of responsibility in the profession.

Furthermore, returning to our previous discussion of the dominance of child development in ECE professional preparation programs, Langford's (2007) study of students in a college program noted that the narrative of the "good" early childhood educator is conceptualized as a universal identity tied to an explicit knowledge of child development. The "bad" educator, though not clearly defined, is inferred as the binary opposite of the good educator. Langford (2007) identifies how knowledge of child development as taught in textbooks is decontextualized from culture. As such, in order to be successful as a "good" educator, students in the study from different cultural backgrounds actively chose to adopt as a central aspect of their epistemological outlook knowledge of child development, knowledge rooted in colonialism and whiteness, which in turn devalues their own (or other) cultural knowledge and ways of being.

This brings us to the most damaging colonial interpretations of equity couched within the discourse of diversity, equity, and inclusion widely taught in ECE professional preparation programs. While on the surface, diversity, equity, and inclusion seem to be reasonable best practices for educators working with different populations, in fact they hide the violence of racist, sexist, classist, ableist, and gendered norms behind an idealized concept of humanity (Todd, 2015). Teaching about diversity generally centres on unexamined and simplistic understandings of culture and language, while inclusion is often subliminally translated in a way that suggests disability. Diversity discourses rarely include conversations about gender, sexuality, and different family compositions (Janmohammed, 2010). Even rarer are critical conversations about race and racism (MacNevin & Berman, 2017). Equity, if it is discussed at all, is often reduced to narrow examples that assume that barriers are inevitable and that we have to figure out how to mitigate them instead of resisting and removing them altogether. Not only are

ECE students taught to apply the logics of diversity, equity, and inclusion discourse—for example, that including "diverse" materials into
their curriculum (such as international play foods) is sufficient—they
are also subject to it. This is, in essence, a double move of inequity.
What are the experiences of ECE students in programs who are considered "diverse"? In an effort to produce good educators well versed
in child development, are we not simultaneously ignoring the intersectionality of ECE students and negating other ways of knowing and
enacting care? This consideration is especially important in the context
of ongoing settler colonialism in Canada. The Truth and Reconciliation Commission and its Calls to Action highlight our responsibility
as educators to enact equity by acknowledging how we are individually
and collectively implicated in ongoing settler colonialism, and they ask
us to actively work toward reconciliation with Indigenous children,
families, and communities.

As public institutions, colleges and universities wield enormous
power to shape public and political discourse through education,
even—perhaps especially—through their silence on care as a political theory. We argue that the ethics of care is sorely needed in ECE
professional preparation programs to enact equity for students within
these programs and beyond into their practice through the disruption
of dominant discourses and the exposure of the binaries and hierarchies
inherent in intersectional forms of oppression that continue to create
and maintain inequity. The question is: How do we begin to incorporate
the ethics of care into ECE professional preparation programs so as to
enact equity? What conditions need to be created to shift the public's
mindset toward *caring with*? As an example of how we might think
with established policy documents, we consider whether the legislated
pedagogical document *How Does Learning Happen? Ontario's Pedagogy
for the Early Years* (*HDLH*) (Ontario Ministry of Education, 2014) offers an opening for (re)thinking equity. As a relational ethics, the ethics
of care aligns with *HDLH* to the extent that the document is focused
on relations, interdependence, and listening. Moreover, *HDLH* invites
educators to question and challenge the status quo (Ontario Ministry of
Education, 2014, p. 13) and to engage in a "rethinking of theories and

practices" (p. 17). We suggest that an ethics of care framework activated through *HDLH*, or other progressive policy or pedagogical documents, offers a way to reassert the value of care in our relations, as well as in the public and political spheres. This opens toward embodied experiences of equity enacted through caring relations with others.

## CONCLUSION

While the term *equity* is increasingly being used in discussions of policy and pedagogy, in this chapter we have resisted the urge to define exactly what equity should look like in early childhood. Instead, we have offered a way to think about equity as something embodied, something that exists when enacted in relations with others. We use the ethics of care to think about what a process of enacting equity may look like in an early childhood setting, with the understanding that equity and care in relations with others must be contextually sensitive and disruptive to existing hierarchies and binaries. We also look to professional preparation programs to reconceptualize equity and disrupt dominant discourses that reproduce the hierarchies and binaries we must contest while enacting equity. To end, we encourage the critical consideration of what happens if we continue to think of equity only as an abstract concept. Will we close ourselves off from the possibility of seeing equity realized in our contexts? We must, then, as early childhood educators, take responsibility and think, and act, otherwise.

## CRITICAL THINKING QUESTIONS

1.  How does thinking about equity as something enacted through an ethics of care benefit your practice in placement settings?
2.  How has your understanding of equity changed after reading this chapter?
3.  What are your experiences of equity in your professional preparation program? Have you been *cared for*?
4.  Where and to what extent do you see equity and ethics of care in your province's early years policy, pedagogy, and program?

## GLOSSARY OF KEY TERMS

**embodied:** Something that is tangible and visible, such as a caring action or the positive feeling a person gets when they are cared for.

**enacted:** A caring value put into action or practice.

**equity in relations:** A way of understanding and thinking about equity as something that exists when created in our multiple relations with others, as opposed to an abstract, rights-based concept.

**ethics of care:** An ethical approach that prioritizes interdependence, care relations, empathy, compassion, recognition of needs, contextual sensitivity, and responsiveness.

**global North, global South:** An alternative to dividing the world into advanced and developing countries.

**master binaries:** Categories, such as male and female, that dominate thinking in our society and that assign value to some categories over others (in this case, male over female).

**neo-colonial hierarchies:** Hierarchies between white people and racialized groups that persist even after a country is no longer a colony.

**paternalism:** The practice among people in authority of deciding what is in the perceived "best interests" of others considered subordinate to them.

**patriarchy:** An external set of rules and values and codes and scripts that specify how men and women should act and be, both in the world and internally. Patriarchy shapes how men and women think and feel, how they perceive and judge themselves, their desires and relationships, and the world they live in (adapted from Gilligan & Snider, 2018, p. 6).

**post-colonial theory:** An intellectual framework that seeks to examine the ways racism and the long-lasting political, economic, and cultural effects of colonialism affect racialized groups in the post-colonial world.

**post-foundational theories:** Ideas, such as ethics of care, that contest and reconceptualize traditional ideas of how our society should work.

# REFERENCES

Engster, D., & Hamington, M. (Eds.). (2015). *Care ethics and political theory.* Oxford University Press.

Fisher, B., & Tronto, J. (1990). Toward a feminist theory of caring. In E. Abel & M. Nelson (Eds.), *Circles of care* (pp. 36–54). SUNY Press.

Gilligan, C. (1982). *In a different voice: Psychological theory and women's development.* Harvard University Press.

Gilligan, C. (2011). *Joining the resistance.* Polity Press.

Gilligan, C., & Snider, N. (2018). *Why does patriarchy persist?* Polity Press.

Hamington, M. (2004). *Embodied care: Jane Adams, Maurice Merleau-Ponty and feminist ethics.* University of Illinois Press.

Hamington, M. (2018). The care ethics moment: International innovations. *International Journal of Care and Caring, 2*(3), 309–318.

Hankivsky, O. (2014). Rethinking care ethics: On the promise and potential of intersectional analysis. *American Political Science Review, 108*(2), 252–264. https://doi.org/10.1017/S0003055414000094

Held, V. (2006). *The ethics of care: Personal, political and global.* Oxford University Press.

Janmohammed, Z. (2010). Queering early childhood studies: Challenging the discourse of developmentally appropriate practice. *Alberta Journal of Educational Research, 56*(3), 304–318.

Kohlberg, L. (1981). *The philosophy of moral development: Moral stages and the idea of justice.* Harper & Row.

Langford, R. (2007). Who is a good early childhood educator? A critical study of differences within a universal professional identity in early childhood education preparation programs. *Journal of Early Childhood Teacher Education, 28*(4), 333–352. https://doi.org/10.1080/10901020701686609

Langford, R. (2010). Critiquing child-centred pedagogy to bring children and early childhood educators into the centre of a democratic pedagogy. *Contemporary Issues in Early Childhood, 11*(1), 113–127. http://dx.doi.org/10.2304/ciec.2010.11.1.113

Langford, R., Richardson, B., Albanese, P., Bezanson, K., Prentice, S., & White, J. (2017). Caring about care: Reasserting care as integral to early childhood education and care practice, politics and policies in Canada. *Global Studies of Childhood, 7*(4), 311–322. https://doi.org/10.1177%2F2043610617747978

MacNevin, M., & Berman, R. (2017). The Black baby doll doesn't fit: The disconnect between early childhood diversity policy, early childhood educator practice, and children's play. *Early Child Development and Care, 187*(5–6), 827–839.

Mooten, N. (2015). Toward a postcolonial ethics of care: In what interest, to regulate what sort of relationships, is the globe evoked? Gayatri Spivak [Unpublished paper]. https://ethicsofcare.org/wp-content/uploads/2016/12/Toward_a_Postcolonial_Ethics_of_Care.pdf

Ontario Ministry of Education. (2014). *How does learning happen? Ontario's pedagogy for the early years.* Ontario Ministry of Education. http://www.edu.gov.on.ca/childcare/HowLearningHappens.pdf

Robinson, F. (2019). Resisting hierarchies through relationality in the ethics of care. *International Journal of Care and Caring, 4*(1), 11–23.

Shewchuk, S., & Cooper, A. (2018). Exploring equity in Ontario: A provincial scan of equity policies across school boards. *Canadian Journal of Education, 41*(4), 917–953.

Spivak, G. (1998). Cultural talks in the hot peace: Revisiting the "global village." In P. Cheah & B. Robbins (Eds.), *Cosmopolitics: Thinking and feeling beyond the nation* (pp. 329–348). University of Minnesota Press.

Todd, S. (2015). Creating transformative spaces in education: Facing humanity, facing violence. *Philosophical Inquiry in Education, 23*(1), 53–61.

Tronto, J. C. (1993). *Moral boundaries: A political argument for an ethic of care.* Routledge.

Tronto, J. C. (2011). Democracy becomes care; care becomes democracy. In C. Leget, C. Gastmans, & M. Verkerk (Eds.), *Care, compassion and recognition: An ethical discussion. Vol. 1: Ethics of care* (pp. 33–49). Peeters Publishers.

Tronto, J. C. (2013). *Caring democracy: Markets, equality and justice.* New York University Press.

van Heijst, A., & Leget, C. (2011). Ethics of care, compassion and recognition. In C. Leget, C. Gastmans, & M. Verkerk, *Care, compassion and recognition: An ethical discussion. Vol. 1: Ethics of care* (pp. 1–14). Peeters Publishers.

CHAPTER 5

# Planning Time for Equity: A (Re)Examination of a Study of ECEs' Perspectives on Planning Time in Southern Ontario

*Lisa Johnston*

## LEARNING OBJECTIVES

- To discuss the entanglements of working conditions, gender, and neoliberalism in the context of equity as praxis
- To describe the tenets of critical qualitative inquiry and what differentiates it from other qualitative approaches
- To acquire a critical awareness by engaging with reconceptualist literature
- To "notice" dominant discourses of developmentalism and neoliberalism in early childhood education spaces
- To "think with" other theoretical frameworks such as those taken up in the reconceptualizing movement

## INTRODUCTION

In this chapter I revisit my master's research paper (Johnston, 2019) on planning time for early childhood educators (ECEs) through the lens of equity as praxis. This research explores ECEs' perspectives on planning time in Southern Ontario. I contend that unpaid planning time is dangerous, first, because a lack of paid planning time negatively affects ECEs' health, well-being, and professional practice, and second, because having paid time to think critically about one's work, subjectivity, and the systems of power that shape and oppress it is potentially dangerous for these very systems. Though I do not explicitly use the idea of equity in my research, I believe it embodies equity as praxis, both in its content and in its process. The concept of praxis, defined by Freire (1970) as "reflection and action upon the world in order to transform it" (p. 51), echoes the ideas of **noticing** and resistance, which I explored in the discussion of my findings. I include the extended quote from Freire here as it speaks directly to my own process of engaging in this research as a form of equity as praxis, and it offers a reference point as I retell the story of my research project:

> Reality which becomes oppressive results in the contradistinction of men as oppressors and oppressed. The latter, whose task it is to struggle for their liberation together with those who show true solidarity, must acquire a critical awareness of oppression through the praxis of this struggle. One of the gravest obstacles to the achievement of liberation is that oppressive reality absorbs those within it and thereby acts to submerge human beings' consciousness. Functionally, oppression is domesticating. To no longer be prey to its force, one must emerge from it and turn upon it. This can be done only by means of the praxis: reflection and action upon the world in order to transform it. (Freire, 1970, p. 51)

## "REALITY WHICH BECOMES OPPRESSIVE ... "

I began my own journey as an early childhood educator in the early 2000s, and I enjoyed a number of blissful years practising this work before the onslaught of professionalization of the early years sector began in Ontario in 2007. Though professionalization was and is a desired goal in the early childhood sector, one that could help ECEs to secure the recognition, respect, and improved wages and working conditions they need and deserve, I am not sure that anyone anticipated the intensification of regulations that would accompany this process. It began with the introduction of a new early learning framework, *Early Learning for Every Child Today* (*ELECT*) (Best Start Expert Panel on Early

Learning, 2007), followed by the establishment of the College of Early Childhood Educators, a regulatory body and the first of its kind for the early childhood workforce. This was followed by placement of the early years sector under the authority of the Ministry of Education in 2010, and, finally, a long overdue renewal of the legislation governing the early years profession, the new Child Care and Early Years Act, in 2014 (Ontario Ministry of Education, 2014a). The year 2014 also saw the revision and truncation of the *ELECT* framework in the form of *Excerpts from "ELECT"* (Ontario Ministry of Education, 2014b) and the introduction of *How Does Learning Happen? Ontario's Pedagogy for the Early Years* (*HDLH*) (Ontario Ministry of Education, 2014c). Amidst all of this, the municipal government in Toronto, where I live and work, replaced its former consultant model of overseeing child-care centres with municipally subsidized spaces with a much more standardized quality-assurance measure known as the *Assessment for Quality Improvement* (*AQI*) (City of Toronto, n.d.). As professionalization proceeded, I, like many others, experienced the growing strain of increasing regulations and expectations without corresponding support (e.g., increased wages and improved working conditions) to meet these expectations. The Association of Early Childhood Educators Ontario (AECEO) has referred to this as the "professionalization gap" (AECEO, n.d.).

This strain was most deeply felt when it came to matters of time. Planning time, whether paid or unpaid, is the only recognized time of the day when educators are supposedly allocated space and time to think about and plan their curriculum programs. Yet this *time* is being consumed by a myriad of other expectations and regulations. Our engagement with children is therefore continually interrupted by outside expectations that shift the focus away from children and toward the need to meet quality-assurance expectations. I needed to get out, to understand, to see this issue from a different perspective, and to gain the language and skills needed to address it and to be heard. So I went back to school.

I knew that my experience was not unique, yet it was difficult to find the evidence. Data on planning time is often buried within quantitative studies of wages and working conditions in both child care (Child Care Sector Human Resources Council, 2013; Doherty et al., 2000; Kipnis et al., 2012; Whitebook & Ryan, 2011) and full-day kindergarten programs in Ontario (Akbari & McCuaig, 2014; Janmohammed et al., 2014; Underwood et al., 2016). I found only two qualitative studies (AECEO, 2016b; Boyd, 2013) that included planning time among the data on working conditions, yet in these studies the voices of ECEs resonated powerfully. Otherwise, the dearth of data about planning time and a lack of representation from ECEs spurred on my study, as did the recognition that ECEs' voices needed to be included in research if they were to have an influence on the policies that directly impact their work (Ryan & Goffin, 2008).

My contention that a lack of planning time is dangerous for ECEs is supported by plentiful research on work stress, job dissatisfaction, frustration, and exhaustion in ECEs (Boyd, 2013; Curbow et al., 2000; Faulkner et al., 2016; Wagner et al., 2013); on depression and burnout in the profession (AECEO, 2017; Blöchliger & Bauer, 2018; Phillips et al., 2016; Roberts et al., 2017); on the negative impacts on ECEs' interactions with children (Phillips et al., 2016); and on higher staff turnover rates (Totenhagen et al., 2016). However, to support my contention that planning time is dangerous because it holds enormous potential as a site of transformation, I required reconceptualist literature (see box 5.1) and a whole new theoretical framework.

## Box 5.1

### Post-Structuralism

Post-structuralism questions the dominant discourses emerging from the Enlightenment, which claim certain truths about the way things are—for example, that men are superior to women. French philosopher Michel Foucault (1979, 1980) referred to dominant discourses as "regimes of truth" that become the accepted way of functioning regardless of whether they are true or not (1980, p. 131), and which use "disciplinary power" and "normalizing technologies" of control to categorize individuals and compare them to universal norms, producing "docile bodies" that do not challenge the status quo. While this may seem bleak, Foucault (1979, 1980) also contended that, where there is power, there is also resistance and freedom.

## ACQUIRING A CRITICAL AWARENESS
## OF OPPRESSION

Halfon and Langford (2015) argue that the issues faced by the predominantly female workforce in early years education are symptomatic of its situation within a neoliberal market system. This prompted me to take up **feminist post-structuralism** as a theoretical framework through which to critically interrogate how the larger discourses of **neoliberalism** and **developmentalism** shape the issue of planning time. Using a feminist post-structural lens, I began to see how planning time is constructed through the organization of time and regulations as normalizing technologies, the subjectivity of the early childhood educator as either good or bad, technician or researcher, and within the relationship between power and resistance.

Briefly, neoliberalism is a masculinized, patriarchal economic system that values competition, individualism, and consumerism. Neoliberalism emerged in the 1970s, as the welfare state began to decline in North America (Davies & Bansel, 2007). Its goal was (and is) to reshape social issues as economic issues by shifting the government's responsibility to look after its citizens to the private market, where individuals must compete to take care of themselves and their own families (Davies & Bansel, 2007). Thus, education has become a neoliberal tool to reproduce future taxpayers, consumers, and entrepreneurs. Neoliberalism's discourses of quality and high returns on investment are readily found in early childhood education, repositioning it as a service and parents as consumers (Moss, 2019) and shaping who ECEs are and how they practice.

Likewise, developmentalism, with its standardized models of child development and developmentally appropriate practice (Bredekamp & Copple, 1997), has become the foundation of early childhood education theory and practice. It is critiqued for its normalization of development in line with white, middle-class, heteronormative standards and its pathologizing of children who do not fit into these universalized norms (Bernhard, 2002; Burman, 1994; Walkerdine, 1988). While theories of child development do offer valuable insights, Moss (2019) contends that developmentalism has become the dominant discourse in early childhood education, shaping our image of the child and the educator, influencing how ECEs practise their craft, and silencing other ways of knowing and being that have the potential to address systemic oppression, racism, and colonialism in Canada (Escayg et al., 2017).

Since neoliberal and developmentalist discourses are the frameworks in which the ECE field is currently invested, feminist post-structuralism provides a useful way of "noticing" and critiquing these discourses, as well as offering ways to name and resist them (MacNaughton, 2005; St. Pierre, 2000). Drawing on Foucault's (1979, 1980) ideas of post-structuralism (see box 5.1), feminist post-structuralism, as theorized by St. Pierre (2000), Osgood (2006), and Cannella (1997), addresses, among other concerns, the concepts of dominant discourse, subjectivity, power, and resistance through a feminist lens. For St. Pierre (2000), examining these discourses means questioning patriarchal power and locating it and the ways it is used to subjectify and oppress women, and indeed everyone. According to Foucault (1979, 1980), dominant discourses employ "normalizing technologies of control" to regulate and thereby shape individuals who then become docile in the face of the power exerted over them, and thus do not resist. Osgood (2006), in her analysis of professionalism in ECE, notices and names these normalizing technologies of control as the "regulatory gaze." We may recognize this as the quality-assurance measures and licensing standards that regulate the ECE profession.

This "regulatory gaze," Osgood (2006) argues, is grounded in masculinized, patriarchal systems. This is problematic, as ECEs' work does not fit neatly into masculinized and patriarchal ideals, nor do ECEs themselves, who are predominantly women, fit these ideals. Yet ECEs are continuously and unknowingly shaped by these norms. This is what is meant by *subjectivity*. Our subjectivities as ECEs are shaped by the dominant discourses in which we live and work—that is, until we notice them. Another way to think about dominant discourses is as stories: the stories through which we learn about what ECE is and how it is to be practised and who ECEs are—all through the lenses of neoliberalism and developmentalism. We often do not realize that these stories are told through powerful systems, or that there are other stories to be told. However, when we do notice the stories and dominant discourses that are shaping and in many ways oppressing ECEs as women working within patriarchal systems, then we can begin to resist and tell our own stories. Resisting requires us to activate our ethical selves (Cannella, 2018) by orienting ourselves toward social justice. The goal is not a complete liberation from power, as St. Pierre (2000) reminds us, but an ongoing daily exercising of resistance within power relations.

With this goal in mind, I explored reconceptualist literature (see box 5.2), using a feminist post-structural lens, to examine how regimes of "clock time" (Kummen, 2010; Pacini-Ketchabaw, 2012; Rose & Whitty, 2010; Wien, 1996; Wien & Kirby-Smith, 1998) and increased regulations (Osgood, 2006) control early childhood settings and are incommensurable with care work that does not easily fit into time that is controlled for efficiency and production (Tronto, 2003). I also explored how regulations construct the image of the educator

---

## Box 5.2

### Reconceptualizing Early Childhood Education

In the late 1970s and early 1980s, theorists in anthropology, psychology, and sociology began to critique the dominant psychology-based discourses of child development, as well as the neoliberal systems that had taken hold in education, giving rise to a growing movement known as the reconceptualizing ECE movement (Bloch et al., 2014). Taking up post-developmental and post-foundational theories such as feminism, critical race theory, queer theory, post-structuralism, and post-colonial and post-human theories, among others, the reconceptualizing ECE movement explored alternative ways to think about, question, and practise early childhood education. In Ontario, *HDLH* uses a reconceptualist lens to re-imagine early childhood education. However, many ECEs are unaware of this positioning and continue to take up and practise *HDLH* through a developmentalist lens.

as a technician (Moss, 2006), applying developmental frameworks, often through the use of checklists, rather than as a researcher who, as envisioned in *HDLH*, engages in critical reflection and collaborative inquiry. Moreover, I probed how the expertise around child development also determines who is recognized as a good educator (Cannella, 1997; Langford, 2007). Finally, I explored calls for resistance in reconceptualist literature. An article by Australian educator-activists Kylie Smith and Sheralyn Campbell (2018) became a road map of resistance for me. Frustrated by the regulatory expectations for standardized documentation of children's learning in individual portfolios, Smith and Campbell make an ethical choice to defy the regulations and instead engage in collective pedagogical documentation of children's learning. They identify these ethical choices as borders of resistance and compliance in their work. I take up this notion here to position planning time as a border of resistance and compliance, a dangerous site of transformation.

## THE PRAXIS OF THIS STRUGGLE

My decision to take up the call to use critical theories to challenge structures and systems of oppression led me to choose critical qualitative inquiry as a methodology (Cannella, 2018; Cannella et al., 2016; Denzin, 2017). Critical qualitative inquiry addresses inequity in both content and process by actively engaging with the oppressed and the systems that oppress them. It ultimately seeks to act in solidarity with participants to bring about change (Cannella, 2018).

I therefore designed a focus group discussion to collect ECEs' perspectives on planning time (Farquhar & Tesar, 2016; Leavy, 2017). All too often ECEs go unheard in staff rooms, so I created a space for their discussions to be heard and recorded. In total, 11 ECEs participated in this study, 9 of whom were part of the focus group discussion, while 2 submitted written responses. All were registered early childhood educators (RECEs). Of the 11 participants, 10 worked in non-profit centres, while 2 had also worked as supervisors and 2 worked as ECEs in full-day kindergarten programs in different school boards. Of all the participants,

6 reported that they worked in unionized settings, including one with two positions: one unionized and one non-unionized. Surprisingly, 7 participants reported that they received paid planning time, though one described this paid planning time as inconsistent. The participants chose their own pseudonyms. They are Molly, DD, DJ, Gina, Frida, Kiana-Monae, Phoebe, Miley, Trisha, DSSD, and Espey D (Johnston, 2019).

The range of contexts represented by the participants attests to the representative nature of the study in that, despite their differences, they agreed that they were all "speaking the same language" (Johnston, 2019). As with all qualitative studies, the results here are contextual and partial, and as such, they are not generalizable. Furthermore, due to time constraints, I was not able to fully enact all of the tenets of critical qualitative inquiry through engaging in direct activism with the participants. This chapter, however, is a continuation of my ongoing commitment to address inequities for ECEs by sharing this research, its theoretical foundations, and by positioning it as a site of activism (MacNaughton, 2005).

## EMERGING FROM AND TURNING UPON OPPRESSION

Following the tenets of critical qualitative inquiry, I engaged directly with ECEs (Cannella, 2018) through an inductive analysis of the participants' discussion, revealing their complex configurations of planning time, the variety and quantity of tasks other than planning that take up their time and cause them stress, their active resistance to these expectations, and a clear demand for what they want and need.

From my own experience, I expected that many of the participants would not have paid planning time, so I was shocked to find that 7 of the 11 participants reported having some form of paid planning time. I worried that this study would not reveal anything if most of the participants had paid planning time. However, I quickly discovered that the complex and varying configurations of planning time they reported in fact provided rich enough detail to suggest a possible ideal configuration that could be offered as a policy recommendation. The configurations of planning time ranged from small amounts, such as 5 to 10 minutes at the beginning and end of the day or a half hour once a week, to more substantial amounts, such as one hour per week or a half hour or even an hour per day. For a while, Molly was paid for a half hour per week during working hours and a half hour per week for working at home, until her union bargained to have that half hour included during working hours. Sharing planning time with a room partner was a key issue for those working in both child care and in full-day kindergarten. Despite having some paid planning time, most of participants described still having to work on their own time; as Molly put it, "It's never enough time. We are all doing it on lunch break. We are all doing it at home. There is just not enough time."

The two participants with the most paid planning time said they felt "lucky" (DJ) and "spoiled" (Phoebe). They reported feeling less stressed, which Phoebe attributed to her reasonable workload and DJ to his workload having been reduced.

Workload was a key theme in the participants' narratives, which revealed the endless expectations and interruptions that take up most of their time, with the documentation of children's learning being the most significant. The Ontario Ministry of Education sets minimum weekly and monthly requirements for program plans and documentation, yet the participants shared how their individual centres doubled or tripled the expectations for documentation, with superiors often invoking the phrase "going above and beyond." As Molly explained,

> We do 20 observations. I have 10 toddlers in my program, we do 20 observations [per week]. Which is not required, but it's required by our centre. And we have said, "No this is way too much." And they say, "No this is what we are doing. We are not doing what other centres are doing. We are doing above and beyond because we are who we are." And you can't get more than a 5 [rating on *AQI*]. No matter what you do, you can only get a 5. So, me doing extra is not going to make a difference. (Johnston, 2019)

But while quotas are used as a standardized measure of quality, Frida explained that they can also undermine quality:

> I can write an observation, a meaningful observation and really pay attention. I engaged with the child. I took the picture. I remember the moment. I had time to write the dialogue if there was dialogue. That is more meaningful than writing 20. (Johnston, 2019)

As noted in the literature, the participants also expressed their feelings of stress related to regulations and the speeding up of the work. Consider the following statements from Gina and Trisha, respectively:

> Our program really isn't reflecting pedagogy or learning through play. It's learning through rules that they have come up with that we need to show that they are learning. That's more stress on us, more stress on the kids, and it's difficult for them. (Johnston, 2019)

> The numbers are an issue in our Kindergarten programs. We have 28, a couple diagnosed, no EA support. It's stressful, and again, it's like you are always planning on the fly. (Johnston, 2019)

To address the expectation that ECEs will do more in less time, centres have begun using apps like HiMama© and Storypark© so ECEs can communicate and share observations of individual children's learning with families in a faster and more convenient manner. However, the participants expressed frustration about the use of technology, which they said required them to spend too much time behind a camera. They also explained that staging pictures and documenting the day's activities in this way actually interrupts children's play. As Kiana-Monae explained,

> The entire day was behind a screen, and that was difficult. I was just communicating with parents, but I felt like the children weren't benefitting, and so I just stopped doing that completely. (Johnston, 2019)

Within her discussion of technology use, Kiana-Monae also demonstrates an act of resistance based on her ethical commitment to the children. Indeed, many of the participants shared stories of ethical resistance to increased regulations and expectations. Some resisted by invoking their job descriptions, which do not specify quotas or forms of documentation, like learning stories. Others pushed back collectively, either as a team or with their unions, to reduce workloads or increase paid planning time. Still, the fear of disciplinary action against individual educators is a reality. Molly described how an inability to meet increased expectations is deemed a "work performance issue" and how she is threatened by her supervisor with being "written up."

The participants in this study not only want daily planning time that is ample, paid, flexible, and undertaken together with their colleagues; they also want to be able to think critically and to have time to really discuss things with their partners, and they want their superiors to revise their expectations of them. The findings modestly suggest that educators should have at least a half hour of paid planning time every day with their team as well as a revision of "above and beyond" expectations. As Espey D asked,

> How is it fair to be held to these incredibly high standards while trying to be taken seriously as educators when we don't have the ample time and resources to complete what's set out before us? (Johnston, 2019)

This sentiment was echoed, first by Miley, and then by Frida:

> Paid programming time is extremely important to me. It contributes to being a professional and allows me to create intentional activities that are researched and that support the learners in my group. Having paid programming time improves my working conditions, allows me to put effort into my planning that truly connects to children, rather than just meeting expectations. (Johnston, 2019)

> Quality is meeting with my colleague and sitting off the floor at least an hour and really discuss, *really discuss*. (Johnston, 2019)

## REFLECTION AND ACTION UPON THE WORLD IN ORDER TO TRANSFORM IT

Continuing with the tenets of critical qualitative inquiry, I shift to engaging indirectly with structures of oppression and positioning this research in the realms of social justice and activism (Cannella, 2018) and as a dangerous site of transformation. I do this by "noticing" the dominant discourses and paradigms of neoliberalism and developmentalism within participants' narratives and by noticing and celebrating the ongoing resistance of the study participants as an embodiment of equity as praxis. I conclude by suggesting tools of resistance readily accessible to all ECEs in Ontario.

Child care's location in a market system means that it is particularly subject to the logics or mechanisms of neoliberalism. By noticing them, educators can help resist them. Molly's response on page 94 allows me to notice how competition, consumerism, and individualization are wound together.

Molly's supervisor responded to her choice to challenge these expectations by saying, "It's a performance issue. If you cannot do it, we will write you up" (Johnston, 2019). In this way, we see that competition is fed by the quality narrative in early childhood education, which parents, as consumers of child-care services, use to make choices about which child-care centre to send their child to. The competitive "going above and beyond" story feeds into consumerism, especially in municipalities like Toronto, where child-care centres' quality-assurance ratings are publicly posted, thereby instigating the doubling and tripling of documentation quotas by centre management. This in turn leads to the speeding up of the work. These "rigid production schedules" (Wien & Kirby-Smith, 1998) are incommensurable with the work of caring for and educating young children (Osgood, 2006; Tronto, 2003). Read Frida's quote again, now through the lens of competition and quality. What do you notice?

> I can write an observation, a meaningful observation and really pay attention. I engaged with the child. I took the picture. I remember the moment. I had time to write the dialogue if there was dialogue. That is more meaningful than writing 20. (Johnston, 2019)

Since neoliberal market systems operate relatively free of government interference, they need ways to maintain their efficiency. One such way is the individualization of the workforce through regulations and disciplinary power. This is evident in Molly's description of challenging her supervisor's expectations that she and her colleagues write 20 observations per week. Her supervisor quickly pushes the individual responsibility for meeting this expectation back on Molly by calling it a "performance issue" and threatening to write her up if she does not comply. This use of disciplinary power maintains this individualizing agenda and even keeps Molly's peers from speaking up in support.

Thus, our subjectivity, who we are as ECEs and how we practise, is shaped by regulations (like quotas and quality-assurance ratings) and disciplinary power (like low scores or being written up), which in turn become "normalizing technologies" of control. As Freire (1970) says, "oppression is domesticating." According to Moss (2006), we become technicians governed by checklists and the application of standardized methods of practice rather than researchers, as we are currently envisioned and positioned in *HDLH*. In *HDLH*, we are expected to engage in critical reflection and collaborative inquiry, and we are invited to question and challenge the status quo—all of which requires time (AECEO, 2016a).

The discourse of developmentalism, with its universalized norms of development and predetermined outcomes supported by checklists, also helps to position ECEs as technicians, and it establishes a narrative of the "good" educator as one with an expertise in child development (Cannella, 1997; Langford, 2007). Thinking with these ideas, what do you notice in this quote by Frida?

> What I don't like is the number, because the number is like picking it out of a hat. Where does this number come from? What does it mean? Why is it 3? Why is it not 4? Why not 2? Right? And show me in my job description that it says 3. It doesn't say. It only says record observations of children. There's no number. By establishing a number also, they stop our creativity. (Johnston, 2019)

Frida not only notices the ways in which the discourses of development-alism and neoliberalism shape her subjectivity as an educator; she also engages in an act of resistance by asking why. It is such acts of resistance that I find most hopeful. Kiana-Monae stops using technology in the classroom because it is interfering with her meaningful engagement with children. Frida refuses to meet "above and beyond" expectations because this is not in her job description and because she feels they are unrealistic. Constrained by the expectation that kindergarten children should be reading by grade 1, Trisha reorders time in her program so as to focus on reading with the children:

> Someday we just decide in the morning, between me and my partner, "Okay, today you are just gonna read. Let the heavens fall down." Unless until there's a fire or somebody's head is cut off, we are gonna read, because we have to send them to grade 1 reading a certain level. And they are expected to sit in their chairs. (Johnston, 2019)

Gina, meanwhile, completes the expectations for learning stories, but according to her own timeline:

> I can't do two observations per month.... I can't work like that. I'm more spontaneous and my work is done, I don't see a problem. (Johnston, 2019)

Yet I find Frida's insistence that "quality comes from us" to be the most powerful act of resistance. It not only rejects external patriarchal measures of quality but reinstates the educator as a central and therefore valuable agent of change. Indeed, it makes Frida, and all of us, dangerous.

## CONCLUSION

Improving wages and working conditions for ECEs requires more than just increasing their paid planning time and revising their workload. It requires a systemic shift in how ECEs and their work are valued and respected, one that can only be brought about through collective resistance to the dominant discourses that currently shape us. I conclude this chapter by calling on ECEs to notice and resist these dominant discourses. I urge us to do a close reading of *HDLH* and to consider the ways this document may be used as a tool of resistance. Noticing how *HDLH* positions ECEs as researchers who are critically reflective and who engage in collaborative inquiry opens up space for us to think and act collectively, to imagine and create new possibilities for ECE programs that respond to our specific contexts and lives. *HDLH* specifically challenges the dominance of developmental discourses in ECE by suggesting that we take up new theories to "think education" otherwise:

> *How Does Learning Happen?* further expands on what we know about child development and invites educators to consider a more complex view of children and the contexts in which they learn and make sense of the world around them. This thinking may require, for some, a shift in mindsets and habits. It may prompt a rethinking of theories and practices—a change in what we pay attention to; in the conversations that we have with children, families, and colleagues; and in how we plan and prepare. (Ontario Ministry of Education, 2014c, p. 17)

Finally, *HDLH* asks us to engage in a "thoughtful questioning and challenging of the status quo on an ongoing basis" in order to "transform programs and bring out the best in children, families, and educators" (Ontario Ministry of Education, 2014c, p. 13). This invitation to question and challenge the status quo is echoed in my own research, and especially in the call to notice and resist embodied in Freire's (1970) provocation to reflect and act on the world in order to transform it. I propose that planning time is just such a time and place for this transformation.

## CRITICAL THINKING QUESTIONS

1. Where do you notice the discourse of neoliberalism in your school or workplace?

2. How does developmentalism limit the possibilities for living well with others?
3. Why is it important to have a critical awareness of oppression?
4. In what ways have you engaged in acts of resistance?
5. Why and how is planning time dangerous?

## GLOSSARY OF KEY TERMS

**developmentalism:** The dominant discourse of child development that forms the foundation of early childhood education theory and practice in North America and the wider English-speaking world.

**feminist post-structuralism:** A theoretical perspective that interrogates the structures of patriarchy in order to name and resist them.

**neoliberalism:** An economic and political system that advances the goals of unlimited economic growth through the power of the free market and limited government regulation.

**noticing:** The dictionary definition of noticing is "to become aware of." It is used here to signal the process of "becoming aware of" the dominant discourses that shape our subjectivities and our work, often in oppressive ways. In order to be able to resist these discourses, we must first notice or become aware of them. I have used the notions of noticing and resisting in the analysis and discussion of my master's research paper. I feel that these notions echo and even embody Freire's (1970) ideas of praxis as "reflection and action upon the world in order to transform it" (p. 51).

## REFERENCES

AECEO [Association of Early Childhood Educators Ontario]. (n.d.). *Professional pay and decent work campaign*. Retrieved January 22, 2021, from https://www.aeceo .ca/professional_pay_decent_work_for_all

AECEO. (2016a). How does learning happen? Inspirational pedagogy in everyday practice depends on a well-supported ECE workforce. *eceLink* (Summer 2016), 6–9. https://www.aeceo.ca/summer_ecelink_2016_now_available_online

AECEO. (2016b). "I'm more than 'just' an ECE": Decent work from the perspective of Ontario's early childhood workforce. *eceLink* (Fall 2016), 6–11. https://d3n8a8pro7vhmx.cloudfront.net/aeceo/pages/941/attachments/original/1476735924/Im_more_than_just_an_ece.pdf?1476735924

AECEO. (2017). *Transforming work in Ontario's early years and child care sector.* Association of Early Childhood Educators Ontario. https://d3n8a8pro7vhmx.cloudfront.net/aeceo/pages/2268/attachments/original/1512010536/AECEO_Recommendations_FinalReport_2017.pdf?1512010536

Akbari, E., & McCuaig, K. (2014). *Early childhood education report 2014.* Ontario Institute for Studies in Education. http://ecereport.ca/media/uploads/pdfs/early-childhood-education-report2014-eng.pdf

Bernhard, J. (2002). Toward a 21st century developmental theory: Principles to account for diversity in children's lives. *Race, Gender & Class, 9*(4), 45–45.

Best Start Expert Panel on Early Learning. (2007). *Early learning for every child today: A framework for Ontario early childhood settings.* Ministry of Children and Youth Services. http://www.edu.gov.on.ca/childcare/oelf/continuum/continuum.pdf

Bloch, M., Swadener, B., & Cannella, G. (2014). Introduction: Exploring reconceptualist histories and possibilities. In M. N. Bloch, B. B. Swadener, & G. Cannella (Eds.), *Reconceptualizing early childhood care and education: Critical questions, new imaginaries and social activism* (pp. 1–16). Peter Lang.

Blöchliger, O. R., & Bauer, G. F. (2018). Correlates of burnout symptoms among childcare teachers: A multilevel modeling approach. *European Early Childhood Education Research Journal, 26*(1), 7–25. https://doi.org/10.1080/1350293X.2018.1412012

Boyd, M. (2013). "I love my work but … " The professionalization of early childhood education. *Qualitative Report, 18*(36), 1–20.

Bredekamp, S., & Copple, C. (1997). *Developmentally appropriate practice in early childhood programs* (Rev. ed.). National Association for the Education of Young Children.

Burman, E. (1994). *Deconstructing developmental psychology.* Routledge.

Cannella, G. S. (1997). *Deconstructing early childhood education: Social justice and revolution.* Peter Lang.

Cannella, G. S. (2018). Critical qualitative research and rethinking academic activism in childhood studies. In M. Bloch, B. Swadener, & G. Cannella, (Eds.), *Reconceptualizing early childhood care and education: A reader: Critical questions, new imaginaries and social activism* (2nd ed., pp. 337–348). Peter Lang.

Cannella, G. S., Pérez, M. S., & Pasque, P. A. (2016). *Critical qualitative inquiry: Foundations and futures.* Left Coast Press.

Child Care Sector Human Resources Council. (2013). *"You bet we still care!" A survey of centre-based early childhood education and care in Canada: Highlights report.* Child Care Human Resources Sector Council. http://www.ccsc-cssge. ca/sites/default/files/uploads/Projects-Pubs-Docs/EN%20Pub%20Chart/ YouBetSurveyReport_Final.pdf

City of Toronto. (n.d.). *Assessment for Quality Improvement (AQI).* Retrieved January 22, 2021, from https://www.toronto.ca/community-people/community-partners/ early-learning-child-care-partners/assessment-for-quality-improvement-aqi/

Curbow, B., Spratt, K., Ungaretti, A., McDonnell, K., & Breckler, S. (2000). Development of the childcare worker job stress inventory. *Early Childhood Research Quarterly, 15*(4), 515–536. https://psycnet.apa.org/doi/10.1016/ S0885-2006(01)00068-0

Davies, B., & Bansel, P. (2007) Neoliberalism and education. *International Journal of Qualitative Studies in Education, 20*(3), 247–259. https://doi.org/10.1080/ 09518390701281751

Denzin, N. K. (2017). Critical qualitative inquiry. *Qualitative Inquiry, 23*(1), 8–16. https://doi.org/10.1080/09518390701281751

Doherty, G., Lero, D., Goelman, H., LaGrange, A., & Tougas, J. (2000). *You bet I care: A Canada-wide study on wages, working conditions and practices in child care centres.* Centre for Families, Work and Well-Being, University of Guelph.

Escayg, K.-A., Berman, R., & Royer, N. (2017). Canadian children and race: Toward an antiracism analysis. *Journal of Childhood Studies, 42*(2), 10–21.

Farquhar, S., & Tesar, M. (2016). Focus groups as temporal ecosystems for newly qualified early childhood teachers. *Contemporary Issues in Early Childhood, 17*(3), 261–274. https://doi.org/10.1177%2F1463949116660949

Faulkner, M., Gerstenblatt, P., Lee, A., Vallejo, V., & Travis, D. (2016). Childcare providers: Work stress and personal well-being. *Journal of Early Childhood Research, 14*(3), 280–293. https://doi.org/10.1177/1476718X14552871

Foucault, M. (1979). *Discipline and punish: The birth of the prison.* Vintage.

Foucault, M. (1980). *Power/knowledge: Selected interviews and other writings, 1972– 1977* (C. Gordon, Ed.). Harvester.

Freire, P. (1970). *Pedagogy of the oppressed.* Seabury Press.

Halfon, S., & Langford, R. (2015). Developing and supporting a high quality child care workforce in Canada: What are the barriers to change? *Our Schools, Our Selves, 24*(4), 131–143.

Janmohammed, Z., McCuaig, K., Akbari, E., Gananathan, R., & Jenkins, J. (2014). *Schools at the centre: Findings from case studies exploring seamless early learning in Ontario.* Atkinson Centre for Society and Child Development at the Ontario Institute for Studies in Education/University of Toronto.

Johnston, L. (2019). *Dangerous time: A critical qualitative inquiry into ECEs' perspectives on planning time in Southern Ontario* [Unpublished master's thesis]. Ryerson University.

Kipnis, F., Whitebook, M., Almaraz, M., Sakai, L., & Austin, L. J. E. (2012). *Learning together: A study of six B. A. completion cohort programs in early care and education. Year 4.* Center for the Study of Child Care Employment, University of California, Berkeley.

Kummen, K. (2010). Is it time to put "tidy up time" away? Contesting routines and transitions in early childhood spaces. In V. Pacini-Ketchabaw (Ed.), *Flows, rhythms, and intensities of early childhood education curriculum* (pp. 97–112). Peter Lang.

Langford, R. (2007). Who is a good early childhood educator? A critical study of differences within a universal professional identity in early childhood education preparation programs. *Journal of Early Childhood Teacher Education, 28*(4), 333–352. https://doi.org/10.1080/10901020701686609

Leavy, P. (2017). *Research design: Quantitative, qualitative, mixed methods, arts-based, and community-based participatory research approaches.* Guilford Press.

MacNaughton, G. (2005). *Doing Foucault in early childhood studies: Applying poststructural ideas.* Routledge.

Moss, P. (2006). Structures, understandings and discourses: Possibilities for re-envisioning the early childhood worker. *Contemporary Issues in Early Childhood, 7*(1), 30–41. https://doi.org/10.2304%2Fciec.2006.7.1.30

Moss, P. (2019). *Alternative narratives in early childhood: An introduction for students and practitioners.* Routledge.

Ontario Ministry of Education. (2014a). *Child Care and Early Years Act.* https://www.ontario.ca/laws/statute/14c11?_ga=1.118789642.285872937.1462810424

Ontario Ministry of Education. (2014b). *Excerpts from "ELECT": Foundational knowledge from the 2007 publication of Early Learning for Every Child Today: A framework for Ontario early childhood settings*. Ontario Ministry of Education. http://www.edu.gov.on.ca/childcare/ExcerptsFromELECT.pdf

Ontario Ministry of Education. (2014c). *How does learning happen? Ontario's pedagogy for the early years*. Ontario Ministry of Education. http://www.edu.gov.on.ca/childcare/HowLearningHappens.pdf

Osgood, J. (2006). Deconstructing professionalism in early childhood education: Resisting the regulatory gaze. *Contemporary Issues in Early Childhood, 7*(1), 5–14. https://doi.org/10.2304%2Fciec.2006.7.1.5

Pacini-Ketchabaw, V. (2012). Acting with the clock: Clocking practices in early childhood. *Contemporary Issues in Early Childhood, 13*(2), 154–160.

Phillips, D., Lea, J. E. Austin, & Whitebook, M. (2016). The early care and education workforce. *The Future of Children, 26*(2), 139–158. doi:10.1353/foc.2016.0016

Roberts, A. M., Gallagher, K. C., Daro, A. M., Iruka, I. U., & Sarver, S. L. (2017). Workforce well-being: Personal and workplace contributions to early educators' depression across settings. *Journal of Applied Developmental Psychology, 61*, 4–12.

Rose, S., & Whitty, P. (2010). "Where do we find the time to do this?" Struggling against the tyranny of time. *Alberta Journal of Educational Research, 56*(3), 257–273.

Ryan, S., & Goffin, S. G. (2008). Missing in action: Teaching in early care and education. *Early Education & Development, 19*(3), 385–395. https://doi.org/10.1080/10409280802068688

Smith, K., & Campbell, S. (2018). Social activism: The risky business of early childhood educators in neoliberal Australian classrooms. In M. Bloch, B. Swadener, & G. Cannella, (Eds.), *Reconceptualizing early childhood care and education: A reader: Critical questions, new imaginaries and social activism* (2nd ed., pp. 313–324). Peter Lang.

St. Pierre, E. A. (2000). Poststructural feminism in education: An overview. *International Journal of Qualitative Studies in Education, 13*(5), 477–515. https://doi.org/10.1080/09518390050156422

Totenhagen, C. J., Hawkins, S. A., Casper, D. M., Bosch, L. A., Hawkey, K. R., & Borden, L. M. (2016). Retaining early childhood education workers: A review of the empirical literature. *Journal of Research in Childhood Education, 30*(4), 585–599. https://doi.org/10.1080/02568543.2016.1214652

Tronto, J. (2003). Time's place. *Feminist Theory, 4*(2), 119–138. https://doi.org/10.1177%2F14647001030042002

Underwood, K., Santo, A. D., Valeo, A., & Langford, R. (2016). Partnerships in full-day kindergarten classrooms: Early childhood educators and kindergarten teachers working together. *Canadian Children, 41*(1), 36–45.

Wagner, S., Forer, B., Cepeda, I., Goelman, H., Maggi, S., D'Angiulli, A., & Grunau, R. (2013). Perceived stress and Canadian early childcare educators. *Child & Youth Care Forum, 42*(1), 53–70. https://doi.org/10.1007/s10566-012-9187-5

Walkerdine, V. (1988) *The mastery of reason: Cognitive development and the production of rationality*. Routledge.

Whitebook, M., & Ryan, S. (2011). *Degrees in context: Asking the right questions about preparing skilled and effective teachers of young children*. National Institute for Early Education Research. http://nieer.org/wp-content/uploads/2016/08/23-2.pdf

Wien, C. A. (1996). Time, work, and developmentally appropriate practice. *Early Childhood Research Quarterly, 11*, 377–403. http://dx.doi.org/10.1016/S0885-2006(96)90013-7

Wien, C. A., & Kirby-Smith, S. (1998). Untiming the curriculum: A case study of removing clocks from the program. *Young Children, 53*(5), 8–13.

# CHAPTER 6

# Using Femme Theory to Foster a Feminine-Inclusive Early Childhood Education and Care Practice

*Adam Davies and Rhea Ashley Hoskin*

## LEARNING OBJECTIVES

- To discuss the ways that the devaluation of femininity is symptomatic of femmephobic societal values, and how femmephobia also informs how ECEC as a field is devalued
- To recognize and reward feminine qualities as part of a highly valued skill set that ought not require masculinization and that contributes significantly to the betterment of ECEC
- To apply femme theory and care ethics to understand how both can inform professional practices in ECEC
- To identify and unpack the cultural tendency to devalue femininity and feminine qualities

## INTRODUCTION

Within the field of early childhood education and care (ECEC)—indeed, in education more broadly—the feminized state of care work has resulted in conversations about purported crises of masculinity

(Martino, 2008; Warin, 2018). This is largely due to the small number of male-identified early childhood educators (ECEs) in the field and the lack of respect for the field of ECEC in general. Subsequently, there have been efforts to "masculinize"[1] the field of ECEC in order to elevate the respect and valuation accorded to ECEs (Warin, 2018). But these efforts to masculinize effectively denigrate femininity by moving the field of ECEC away from care through notions of **professionalization** and standardization, while also reifying pre-existing gendered hierarchies that privilege men and masculinity over women and femininity (Martino, 2008; Hoskin, 2019b). **Masculinization** discourses encourage men who work in the field of ECEC to emphasize traditionally masculinized traits (e.g., assisting in the development of children's leadership skills) while de-emphasizing the role that care plays in their job and disassociating themselves from femininity (Warin, 2018).

Rather than masculinize, as the literature suggests, what if efforts were made to value femininity instead? A growing area of inquiry has attended to the cultural (de)devaluing of femininity: critical femininities and femme theory. Following Middleton (2019), in this chapter we ask what it would be like to curate a space wherein femininity was valued and embraced. This, a central question of femme theory (Hoskin, 2017a, 2019a), guides us in revisioning a feminine-positive space as a means of dislodging the naturalized femmephobia (i.e., the societal devaluation and regulation of femininity) embedded within current ECEC efforts to "masculinize" or otherwise offset "feminization." This chapter promotes a feminine-inclusive ECEC practice that embraces and affirms femininity in the field of ECEC. Applying **femme theory**, we engage with how femininity can be centralized and operationalized in ECEC by shifting conversations from a focus on biological sex and **gender essentialism** to affirmative constructions of femininity. Importantly, we distinguish sex (female, male, intersex, etc.), gender/sex (woman, man, non-binary, etc.), and gender (femininity, masculinity, androgyny, etc.; see van Anders, 2015). This chapter begins by delineating three key theoretical frameworks—femme theory, the ethics of care, and care theory—and then examines how each, in turn, aids in the reconsideration of femininity within ECEC.

## FEMME THEORY

Historically, the term *femme* has referred to feminine lesbians who align themselves with butch lesbians (Nestle, 1992). However, with the queering of gender/sex categories has come a plurality of femme identities and expressions (Blair & Hoskin, 2015; Davies, 2020). This multiplicity has propped up the nascent femme concept as a theoretical framework (Hoskin, 2017a, 2019a). Femme theory challenges and illuminates the centrality of masculine epistemologies (Hoskin, 2019a; Schwartz, 2018)—namely, by rethinking how femininity is (de)valued and examining femininity within gendered economies, power, and hegemony (Hoskin, 2020). Of particular relevance, femme theory offers an analytical framework that centres both femininity and feminine devaluation (Hoskin, 2019a). Additionally, femme theory posits that associations between femininity and inferiority are pervasive and deeply ingrained, and in this way makes femininity integral to understanding—or reimagining—systems of power and inequality (Hoskin, 2019a, 2019b).

Femme theory has been a useful theoretical framework through which to analyze feminist pedagogies (Bimm & Feldman, 2020; Hoskin, 2017b), in-group discrimination (Blair & Hoskin, 2015), and popular cultural texts (Hoskin & Taylor, 2019). Of particular relevance here, femme theory has tangentially explored ideas of professionalism. For instance, participants in Hoskin's (2019b) study described professionalism as a masculine arena and talked about needing to "masculinize" their gender aesthetic in order to be taken seriously as intelligent, credible professionals.

This finding is echoed by femme and critical femininities scholarship, in which notions of authenticity as a masculine domain are frequently found to undermine feminine subjecthood (Davies, 2020; Hoskin, 2020). This body of work highlights the fact that masculinity is seen as authentic, which, in comparison to femininity, bolsters both respectability and professionalism. Researchers have found this to be the case across sexual orientations and gender identities, particularly for gay men (Davies, 2020), lesbians (Blair & Hoskin, 2015), and non-binary people (Hoskin, 2019b, 2020), as well as within the field of ECEC, where care work is devalued and degendered under **neoliberal** individualistic policy approaches (Bezanson, 2017). Schwartz (2018) and Hoskin (2017a, 2019a) draw on femme theory to understand the tendency to overlook femininity and consider it invalid or illegitimate.

Like other femme scholars, they argue that this tendency is a product of a reigning masculine norm that renders femininity perpetually inferior: if masculinity is normal, neutral, and natural, femininity is, by contrast, other, artificial, and inauthentic (Davies, 2020; Hoskin, 2020). The positioning of femininity as inauthentic begs the question: If femininity is not taken seriously, is not seen as genuine but only as fake, deceptive, or unintelligent, how can we ever begin to see femininity as something of value, or even as a professional virtue?

## THE ETHICS OF CARE

Care is highly valued within ECEC policy. For example, the prioritization of care is reflected in the Ontario College of Early Childhood Educators' (2017) Code of Ethics, which outlines "the profession's core set of beliefs and values of care, respect, trust and integrity" (p. 7). With "care" being a central tenet of the field of ECEC (Warin, 2018), there remains uncertainty about how to centralize care in ECEC. Langford et al. (2020) ask, "What might ECEC policy, politics and practice in Canada be like if an ethics of care was central to each of them?" (p. 110). An ethics of care refers to "the compelling moral salience of attending to and meeting the needs of particular others for whom we take responsibility" (Held, 2006, as cited in Langford et al., 2020, p. 110).

The ethics of care, broadly speaking, moves away from universalized principles governing interactions and toward contextual, relational, and interpersonal ethics (Sander-Staudt, 2018), with a specific focus on the relationship between the care provider (for example, ECEs) and the cared-for (for example, children) (Noddings, 1984). Despite the prominence of "care" in ECEC frameworks (Ontario Ministry of Education, 2014a, 2014b), professionalization paradoxically coincides with masculinization to ensure ECEC's legitimacy (Martino, 2008; Warin, 2018). The tendency to (re)value things coded as feminine through masculinization is heavily criticized by femme scholars, who urge researchers to consider how femininity can be valued on its own terms (Hoskin, 2019a).

While our analysis separates gender and sex as constructs, both have a shared history and can overlap in normative ways (van Anders, 2015). Thus, an effort to masculinize (e.g., gender and masculinity) can take up tools of sexism (e.g., male superiority) to accomplish its goal. For example, many efforts have been made to recruit more men as registered early childhood educators (RECEs) into the field, with 1,026 of 55,719 RECEs in Ontario self-identifying as men as of December 31, 2019 (Ontario College of Early Childhood Educators, 2019). In 2016, the Ontario College of Early Childhood Educators published a report entitled "Gaining a Better Understanding of Men in Early Childhood Education," in which it emphasized "the importance of boisterous, vigorous and very physical play that men may engage in easily" (para. 5). The gender essentialist notions that connect these qualities to men are not new. Rather, such notions re-inscribe a binary view of men and women that denigrates the more "feminized" aspects of ECEC commonly associated with women (such as "care" and "nurturance").

What is most striking about this effort is how sexist and femmephobic ideologies are deployed to secure more men in the field of ECEC. This begins first by creating a binary between gender and sex (e.g., men are masculine in specific desirable ways) and secondly, by inferring that the qualities associated with women—femininity—are of less importance. Operating in tandem, processes of gender essentialism, sexism, and femmephobia underscore initiatives to masculinize the field. Thus, it is not only care discourses that must be revalued within an ECEC context, but also constructions of femininities more broadly. Within the field of ECEC, femininity is devalued through efforts to "professionalize," most notably via recruitment efforts to bring more male ECEs into the field (Warin, 2018). By challenging the gendered relations that re-inscribe men and masculinity as being of more value in the field, this analysis disrupts how **femmephobia** presents itself within gender hierarchies in ECEC. Rather than reproducing gender hierarchies, an ECEC practice informed by femme theory seeks to cultivate a place where femininity is valued and embraced.

## CARE THEORY

Care theory applies a feminine moral approach to **care ethics** in order to centralize the interdependence of human relationships (Gilligan, 1982; Noddings, 1984; Sander-Staudt, 2018). Predominantly focusing on the relationships between a **care provider** and the **cared-for**, care theory centralizes a dynamic that is based upon the care provider's ability to be self-reflexive and responsive to the needs of the cared-for (Kittay, 2015; Noddings, 1984). Importantly, care theory, given the masculinist foundations of liberal legal theories, does not always centralize individual human rights as a framework (Gilligan, 1982; Noddings, 1984; Sander-Staudt, 2018). While care theories are common in feminist ethical debates, they are not always seen as distinctly feminist since some liberal feminist theorists have criticized care theories for being gender essentialist, less political than liberal feminist approaches, and universalist (Sander-Staudt, 2018). However, we find that the additional delineation of sex and gender noted above (van Anders, 2015) offers a layer of nuance to care theory that mitigates the threat of gender essentialism.

Care theory is central in many fields in which there is a dynamic between the care provider and the cared-for, particularly in relation to "feminine ethics" (Gilligan, 1982; Noddings, 1984). Carol Gilligan (1982) first theorized "feminine ethics" as a way to consider the moral development of girls and women through relationality and as a critique of psychologist Lawrence Kohlberg's privileging of moral autonomy and independence. Critiquing legal ethics and individualistic approaches to psychology, a feminine ethics of care seeks to see relationships between humans as moral frameworks instead of liberal contractual theories, which are often critiqued for their masculinist perspectives (Sander-Staudt, 2018). Nel Noddings (1984) expanded on the theorization of "care" by articulating the importance of a feminine ethic that values interdependency and relationality in education.

At the same time, and as noted above, care theories have been critiqued for being gender essentialist in nature. For example, Sander-Staudt (2018) delineates the ways in which care has been traditionally associated with motherhood (particularly white motherhood), and she shows that the relationship between sex and gender in care ethics and theories remains tumultuous (see also Abawi et al., 2019). Gender essentialist discourses are particularly salient in ECEC, where normative ideas of motherhood and nurturance still contribute to the purported feminization of the field and the low number of male educators within it (Warin, 2018). These discourses reify the stereotype that ECEC is "women's work" and that women are more naturally inclined to perform labours of care and nurturance.

Unfortunately, rather than engaging with harmful essentialist views of gender by showing how work coded as feminine *is* important and that femininity is a quality worth aspiring to, ECEC has commonly advocated for masculinization and neoliberal ideals such as standardization and the importation of pedagogical approaches used in primary education (i.e., teacher-directed instruction)—goals that reify both essentialist gender ideology and feminine inferiority (Dahlberg et al., 1999). The deployment of "femininity" as a trait essential to women can also reinforce notions that women are biologically determined as better caregivers than men, and that ECEC should therefore only be occupied by those who identify as women. Equally, this process reinforces the idea that men with feminine qualities are unnatural, a norm that bolsters masculinity's repudiation of femininity (Davies, 2020).

To this end, *feminist ethics* and *feminine ethics* are often conflated with one another despite the fact that feminine ethics concerns itself with "aspects of traditional Western ethics that devalue female moral experiences" (Houser et al., 2006, p. 40). This conflation is relevant since research has described the devaluation of ECEC on both an individual scale, as reflected by hourly wages, and a community level in terms of societal recognition (Kim & Reifel, 2010). Interestingly, Barton and Huebner (2020) note how tasks, skills, or traits that are seen as falling within a "women's domain" are automatically constructed as trivial. These authors note how "the very fact that a *woman* does something, much less does so better than a man, devalues the skill within patriarchy. Such a formulation ensures that Westerners never perceive feminine ways of power as compelling, effective, and something to emulate" (Barton & Huebner, 2020, p. 3). Likewise, efforts to professionalize the field of ECEC through managerial approaches often accompany an attempt to masculinize the field by de-emphasizing care as a moral approach (Warin, 2018). We must consider these efforts while also making connections to the wider scale of society's devaluation of femininity.

## CARE THEORY AND EARLY CHILDHOOD EDUCATION AND CARE

Care is a central component of ECEC, with many early year Canadian curricular documents focusing on care as a facet of ECEC work (e.g., Ontario Ministry of Education, 2014a, 2014b). Here, care is operationalized as providing a "*substitute* home reproducing, as closely as possible, the model of maternal care" (Dahlberg et al., 1999, pp. 63–64). Thus, ECEs must manage the expectation to reproduce gender essentialist notions of maternal care and mothering due to economic conditions that demand all parental figures work outside of the home (Dahlberg et al., 1999). Thus, the goal of ECEC often lies in reproducing the feminized *feeling* of nurturance that society traditionally places upon mothers while allowing mothers to work outside the home (Dahlberg et al., 1999).

Within Western society, **dependency** is considered a feminized state of weakness, particularly under masculinist socio-political structures that encourage self-reliance, self-sufficiency, and independence. To be emotionally, physically, financially, or politically dependent is thought to reflect a lack of normative functioning, a failure in the face of neoliberal demands for complete autonomy and self-reliance. As Kittay (2015) describes, care providers are often placed in conditions of enforced dependency in which their needs and desires are placed below those in their care. Moreover, workers' emotional and physical labours—although necessary to assist those deemed vulnerable in society—are often undervalued and not equitably compensated.

Care work is associated with emotional labour and ensuring the comfort and ease of others (Josephidou & Bolshaw, 2020). Making connections between nursing and ECEC, Josephidou and Bolshaw (2020) note how nursing has worked toward "gender balance" in terms of the gender identities of its workforce, while ECEC has yet to achieve such a balance. Still, it is important to interrogate *why* the necessity remains to encourage men to enter the field of ECEC, and *which traits* assumed inherent to men they are anticipated to bring into the field. Warin (2018) distinguishes between discourses of "gender balance" and "gender flexibility" in ECEC. Gender balance, in this explanation, refers to the notion that men and women carry distinct and unique traits that they bring to care work with children, meaning that by achieving a gender balance, the field of ECEC might be able to have a more equal amount of normative gender roles and influences in the field. This argument is commonly used in efforts to recruit more men into ECEC since it is thought that more traditionally male roles and influences will be brought into the field through the physical presence of more men.

Warin (2018), drawing from French post-structuralist theorizations of gender, advocates for gender flexibility instead of gender balance per se. In this theorization, gender is fluid, shifting, and non-binary, with practitioners of all gender identities being willing to occupy varying gender roles with an explicitly gender egalitarian and equitable male workforce who do not necessarily reinforce dominant constructions of masculinity. For example, the notion that men can serve as "role models" by bringing more masculine activities into the realm of ECEC continues to devalue femininity through gender essentialist logics (Warin, 2018). Martino (2008) describes how calls for male role models in elementary education play on "**recuperative masculinity politics**" (Lingard & Douglas, 1999) that seek to counteract the "feminization" of schooling and cultivate more "boy friendly" and "active" learning spaces. We argue that these politics are widespread within ECEC, and that the logics underscoring such politics are not only problematic for their construction of masculinity and gender essentialism but also for sexist and femmephobic platforms.

## THE MASCULINIZATION AND PROFESSIONALIZATION OF ECEC

The masculinization of ECE work links professionalism discourses to dominant constructions of masculinities (Martino, 2008). According to Maher (2012), the (re)masculinization of teaching and education is commonly depicted through two threads: (1) the traditional streamlining of women into the field of teaching and its position as "women's work," and (2) the feminization of the field, which positions the field of teaching as less rigorous, less demanding, and less respected. Maher (2012) questions the embedded sexism within the term *feminization*, as it indicates a devaluation and de-professionalization of a field that is historically and currently dominated by women and feminine-coded labour. However, such a challenge to the term *feminization of teaching* still leaves intact the notion that to be feminine is *inherently* negative, and that by changing the term, perhaps, the field will not be seen as feminine and, in turn, will become valued.

This denigration of care work and its associations with femininity and "women's work" operates through femmephobic discourses that essentialize the connection between femininity and womanhood while reproducing both sexism and femmephobia. Similar discourses are deployed in efforts to recruit more men into teaching and ECEC, which seek to both regulate and discipline current male workers' diverse gendered subjectivities (Martino, 2008). While previous research has connected such regulatory mechanisms, research has yet to make explicit links between masculinization and femmephobia, particularly in ECEC.

## VALUING CARE THROUGH A FEMININITY-AFFIRMATIVE LENS AND PEDAGOGIES

In the professional practise of ECEC, care is emphasized as a core component of pedagogy, yet little is provided to assist practitioners in understanding how to embed care within their everyday practices.

What is missing is an understanding of how to *value care through a femininity-affirmative lens and critical pedagogy*. **Critical pedagogy** involves an emancipatory pedagogical approach that focuses on social transformation, challenging hegemonic structures—such as racism, sexism, heterosexism, and ableism—by illuminating how structures of education are embedded within dominant frameworks that marginalize and oppress students (Freire, 1970; Kridel, 2010). While critical pedagogy provides a lens through which we can consider social change and challenge hegemonic structures through everyday pedagogical approaches, it has been criticized for focusing on a masculinized active subject, which, as Sheldon (2017) articulates, "constructs passivity and receptivity as unilaterally negative," which in turn leads to an "overall devaluing of anything passive and receptive, characteristics which are traditionally associated with femininity" (p. 91). While this critique is located in the K–12 school setting, we expand upon critiques of the masculinism within critical pedagogy and bring the conversation into ECEC to argue for a femininity-affirmative pedagogical approach that values care and relational practices. Instead of considering social transformation through activeness or the transgression of norms, social change can take place through practices of care and relationality, with a specific space made for the valuation of femininity.

Given femme's articulation as the refusal to approximate the patriarchal norms of femininity (Hoskin, 2017a, 2017b; Hoskin & Taylor, 2019), femme as an intervention into ECEC symbolizes a refusal to approximate cultural and disciplinary norms that privilege masculinity. For example, Bimm and Feldman (2020) theorize a femme pedagogy for care work as prioritizing relationality, compassion, and communal practices by working against the "individualist, neoliberal rhetoric of grit and toughness" (n.p.). Within the context of ECEC, femme provides the tools to highlight the tendency to valorize qualities coded as masculine. Thus, as a pedagogical and theoretical mode, femme asks us to consider how qualities and characteristics deemed feminine exist in us all, and how those qualities wield transformational capabilities (Bimm & Feldman, 2020; Hoskin, 2019a). Applying femme theory within the context of ECEC, and in line with Bimm and Feldman (2020), we see femme pedagogy as pushing back against concerns about being "too soft," and focusing instead on changing the surrounding world to value softness.

## CONCLUSION

The masculinization of ECEC not only connects to broader structures of sexism and femmephobia, it also undercuts one of the foundational principles of the field: care. In recognition of the discrepancy between masculinization efforts and the core principles of ECEC, we propose using femme theory to incorporate analyses of femmephobia into existing frameworks for ECEC and care ethics. Through the incorporation of an analytical approach that considers how femmephobia is embedded within efforts to professionalize and masculinize ECEC, as well as efforts to recruit men into the field, more space can be cultivated for gender diversity in all its forms. Equally, such an approach could allow us to generate the valuation of care work at a systemic level by embracing relations and productions of femininities.

## NOTE

1.   Scholars, such as Martino (2008) and, originally, Lingard and Douglas (1999), discuss the "re-masculinization" of schooling in the context of policy attempts to recruit men to elementary education and the seeming decline in male elementary educators and the perceived crisis of masculinity in the field. While we acknowledge this important usage of the term, we contextualize our work in ECEC and use the term *masculinization* to refer more generally to gendered attempts to devalue and diminish constructs and relations of femininities in ECEC while being in conversation with literature on "re-masculinization" in schooling broadly.

## CRITICAL THINKING QUESTIONS

1.   How can we cultivate a feminine-affirmative pedagogical approach that values tasks, skills, or traits coded as feminine and allows them to be nurtured across identities, whether those of men, women, or non-binary people?

2. How can we embrace femininity and feminine labour as the bedrock of ECEC without attempting to use masculinity to revalue labour itself?
3. How are femmephobic "tools" deployed to accomplish particular goals within and outside of ECEC? What are some examples of femmephobia in your day-to-day life?

## GLOSSARY OF KEY TERMS

**care ethics:** An ethical approach and theoretical framework that values interpersonal ethics, relationality, and contextual decision making instead of universalized legal approaches (Sander-Staudt, 2018). Originally theorized by Gilligan (1982) and Noddings (1984) to challenge the masculinism within male-centred moral psychological frameworks.

**care provider:** The employee, such as a personal support worker or early childhood educator, providing care for a specific population.

**cared-for:** Those in the position of receiving care from a worker for everyday survival.

**critical pedagogy:** A pedagogical approach that focuses on teaching and how to critically prepare educators for mass change by challenging dominant structures and systems of marginalization in society.

**dependency:** The degree to which an individual might be physically, emotionally, financially, or otherwise reliant upon other individuals and/or state institutions in their everyday life for survival.

**femmephobia:** The systemic denigration and regulation of femininity that operates through gendered norms and hierarchies (i.e., femininity's subordinated status) (Hoskin, 2020).

**femme theory:** A theoretical framework used to illuminate femininity as an intersectional axis. Femme theory challenges the deeply ingrained assumptions about feminine inferiority and is concerned with the systemic devaluation and regulation of femininity (i.e., femmephobia). Moreover, it views femininity as integral to understanding social inequalities and issues of power (Hoskin, 2017a, 2019a).

**gender essentialism:** The notion that women and men hold inherent biological traits that result in their essential difference; using biological sex as a determinant for one's gender.

**masculinization:** The notion that a certain field (such as ECEC) is looking for male influences to encourage more men to enter the field.

**neoliberalism:** An economic structure developed throughout the twentieth century that treats the individual as the central unit of analysis and encourages decision making through economic rationalities and the dissolution of social relations through hyper-individualism.

**professionalization:** A discourse that focuses upon standardization and evaluation criteria, and which attempts to de-emphasize relationships and care in ECE.

**recuperative masculinity politics:** A rejection of the feminist politics that seeks gender equality. Such politics present dominant constructs of masculinity as "at risk"—a view frequently forwarded by men's rights groups (Lingard & Douglas, 1999).

## REFERENCES

Abawi, Z., Berman, R., & Powell, A. (2019). Gender, race, and precarity: Theorizing the parallels between early childhood educators and sessional faculty in Ontario. *Atlantis: Critical Studies in Gender, Culture & Social Justice/Atlantis: études critiques sur le genre, la culture, et la justice, 40*(1), 45–60.

Barton, B., & Huebner, L. (2020). Feminine power: A new articulation. *Psychology & Sexuality*. https://doi.org/10.1080/19419899.2020.1771408

Bezanson, K. (2017). Mad Men social policy: Families, social reproduction, and childcare in a conservative Canada. In R. Langford, S. Prentice, & P. Albanese (Eds.), *Caring for children: Social movements and public policy in Canada* (pp. 9–36). UBC Press.

Bimm, M., & Feldman, M. (2020, January 27). Toward a femme pedagogy, or making space for trauma in the classroom. *MAI: Feminism and Digital Culture*. https://maifeminism.com/towards-a-femme-pedagogy-or-making-space-for-trauma-in-the-classroom/

Blair, K. L., & Hoskin, R. A. (2015). Experiences of femme identity: Coming out, invisibility and femmephobia. *Psychology & Sexuality, 6*(3), 229–244.

Dahlberg, G., Moss, P., & Pence, A. R. (1999). *Beyond quality in early childhood education and care: Postmodern perspectives.* Psychology Press.

Davies, A. W. (2020). "Authentically" effeminate? Bialystok's theorization of authenticity, gay male femmephobia, and personal identity. *Canadian Journal of Family and Youth/Le Journal Canadien de Famille et de la Jeunesse, 12*(1), 104–123.

Freire, P. (1970). *Pedagogy of the oppressed.* Bloomsbury.

Gilligan, C. (1982). *In a different voice: Psychological theory and women's development.* Harvard University Press.

Held, V. (2006). *The ethics of care: Personal, political and global.* Oxford University Press.

Hoskin, R. A. (2017a). Femme interventions and the proper feminist subject: Critical approaches to decolonizing contemporary Western feminist pedagogies. *Cogent Open Access Social Sciences, 3*(1), 1–17.

Hoskin, R. A. (2017b). Femme theory: Refocusing the intersectional lens. *Atlantis: Critical Studies in Gender, Culture & Social Justice, 38*(1), 95–109.

Hoskin, R. A. (2019a). Can femme be theory? Exploring the epistemological and methodological possibilities of femme. *Journal of Lesbian Studies.* https://doi.org/10.1080/10894160.2019.1702288

Hoskin, R. A. (2019b). Femmephobia: The role of anti-femininity and gender policing in LGBTQ+ people's experiences of discrimination. *Sex Roles, 81*, 686–703.

Hoskin, R. A. (2020). "Femininity? It's the aesthetic of subordination": Examining femmephobia, the gender binary, and experiences of oppression among sexual and gender minorities. *Archives of Sexual Behavior.* https://www.tandfonline.com/doi/full/10.1080/10894160.2019.1702288

Hoskin, R. A., & Taylor, A. (2019). Femme resistance: The fem(me)inine art of failure. *Psychology & Sexuality, 10*(4), 281–300.

Houser, R., Wilczenski, F. L., & Ham, M. (2006). *Culturally relevant ethical decision-making in counseling.* SAGE Publications.

Josephidou, J., & Bolshaw, P. (2020). *Understanding gender and early childhood: An introduction to the key debates.* Routledge.

Kim, M., & Reifel, S. (2010). Child care teaching as women's work: Reflections on experiences. *Journal of Research in Childhood Education, 24*(3), 229–247.

Kittay, E. (2015). Dependence. In R. Adams, B. Reiss, & D. Serlin (Eds.), *Keywords in disability studies* (pp. 54–58). New York University Press.

Kridel, C. (Ed.). (2010). *Encyclopedia of curriculum studies.* (Two volumes). SAGE Publications.

Langford, R., Powell, A., & Bezanson, K. (2020). Imagining a caring early childhood education and care system in Canada: A thought experiment. *International Journal of Care and Caring, 4*(1), 109–115.

Lingard, B., & Douglas, P. (1999). *Men engaging feminisms: Profeminism, backlashes and schooling.* Open University Press.

Maher, F. A. (2012). Feminization of teaching. In J. A. Banks (Ed.), *Encyclopedia of diversity in education* (pp. 901–905). SAGE Publications.

Martino, W. (2008). Male teachers as role models: Addressing issues of masculinity, pedagogy and the re-masculinization of schooling. *Curriculum Inquiry, 38*(2), 189–223.

Middleton, M. (2019, Fall). Feminine exhibition design. *Exhibition,* 82–91. https://b033418d-11a7-49a3-bbde-c0d18406843d.filesusr.com/ugd/ae50a5_888321fb4009401c84c688113aeb42d4.pdf?index=true

Nestle, J. (Ed.). (1992). *The persistent desire: A femme-butch reader.* Alyson Books.

Noddings, N. (1984). *Caring: A relational approach to ethics and moral education.* University of California Press.

Ontario College of Early Childhood Educators. (2016, April 20). *Gaining a better understanding of men in early childhood education* [Press release]. https://www.college-ece.ca/en/public/news/gaining-a-better-understanding-of-men-in-early-childhood-education

Ontario College of Early Childhood Educators. (2017). *Code of ethics and standards of practice for registered Ontario early childhood educators in Ontario.* Ontario College of Early Childhood Educators. https://www.college-ece.ca/en/Documents/Code_and_Standards_2017.pdf

Ontario College of Early Childhood Educators. (2019). *Fair registration practices report.* Ontario College of Early Childhood Educators. https://www.college-ece.ca/en/Documents/Fair_Registration_Practices_Report_2019.pdf

Ontario Ministry of Education. (2014a). *Excerpts from "ELECT": Foundational knowledge from the 2007 publication of Early Learning for Every Child Today: A framework for Ontario early childhood settings.* Ontario Ministry of Education. http://www.edu.gov.on.ca/childcare/ExcerptsFromELECT.pdf

Ontario Ministry of Education. (2014b). *How does learning happen? Ontario's pedagogy for the early years.* Ontario Ministry of Education. http://www.edu.gov.on.ca/childcare/HowLearningHappens.pdf

Sander-Staudt, M. (2018). Care ethics. In *Internet encyclopedia of philosophy.* https://www.iep.utm.edu/care-eth/

Schwartz, A. (2018). Locating femme theory online. *First Monday, 7*(2). https://doi
.org/10.5210/fm.v23i7.9266

Sheldon, J. (2017). The pedagogy of the student: Reclaiming agency in receptive
subject-positions. *Journal of Curriculum Theorizing, 32*(1). https://journal
.jctonline.org/index.php/jct/article/view/681

van Anders, S. (2015). Beyond sexual orientation: Integrating gender/sex and diverse
sexualities via sexual configurations theory. *Archives of Sexual Behavior, 44*(5),
1177–1213. https://doi.org/10.1007/s10508-015-0490-8

Warin, J. (2018). *Men in early childhood education and care: Gender balance and
flexibility.* Springer.

# CHAPTER 7

# Making Space for Indigenous Knowledge in an Urban Child-Care Centre

*Maya-Rose Simon*

## LEARNING OBJECTIVES

- To discuss the importance of the long-standing and more recent call for culturally appropriate early childhood education in Indigenous communities in Canada
- To recognize that Indigenous knowledge will not be successful in mainstream education if it is looked at as separate or an add-on to the current curriculum
- To identify Indigenous knowledge and pedagogy and their potential benefits for all children

## INTRODUCTION

I would like to begin this chapter by acknowledging the land on which I currently live and work: the traditional territory of the Mississaugas of the New Credit First Nation. I am a guest in this space, and I share an obligation to respect, honour, and sustain this land.

The Truth and Reconciliation Commission of Canada (TRC) investigated the involvement of the Canadian government and various religious organizations in the removal of First Nation, Métis, and Inuit children from their families and communities for the purpose of educating them in residential schools (Truth and Reconciliation Commission of Canada, 2015). The Canadian government, under the **Indian Act**, forcefully removed Indigenous children from their homes and placed them in schools operated by religious organizations. The TRC enabled survivors to bear witness to the impact Indian residential schools had on their lives, their families, and their communities (Truth and Reconciliation Commission of Canada, 2015).

The TRC developed 94 Calls to Action for Canadians, an entire section of which were dedicated to education (Truth and Reconciliation Commission of Canada, 2015). One calls for "**culturally appropriate early childhood education programs**" (Truth and Reconciliation Commission of Canada, 2015, p. 205). The call for early childhood education (ECE) programs is significant, for it speaks to Indigenous ways of being. In Indigenous cultures, children play a fundamental role in the well-being of the community (Royal Commission on Aboriginal Peoples, 1996). The TRC's final report emphasized the vital role early childhood programs play in fostering child development and rebuilding communities, thereby recognizing the Indigenous view of the child and the power children possess (Truth and Reconciliation Commission of Canada, 2015, p. 205). The TRC Calls to Action urge Canadians to make space for Indigenous people, knowledge, ways, and practices.

In this chapter, I first locate myself and the context in which I live. I then discuss colonial education, ECE programs in First Nations and Inuit communities, Indigenous knowledge, and land-based pedagogy. These sections will be followed by the presentation and discussion of a qualitative research study that explored the effects on children and teachers when space is made for Indigenous knowledge and practices in an urban child-care centre. The chapter concludes with some recommendations to support the call for culturally appropriate ECE programs.

## MY INDIGENOUS IDENTITY

As a member of the Anishinaabe, Chippewa Nation, and Métis I have been directly affected by the Canadian and US government policies on Indigenous Peoples. In Canada, I am subjected to the Indian Act of 1876 and in the United States, the Indian Reorganization Act of 1934, which determines blood quantum. These two pieces of legislation have impacted my identity and my traditional knowledge. Lawrence (2003) discusses how Indigenous identity is consistently being negotiated in relation to laws defining and controlling "Indianness" (Simon, 2017). These laws have distorted and disrupted Indigenous ways of self-identifying.

Métis are the offspring of an Indigenous person and a settler in Canada. Métis are constantly being asked to define their identity. Métis developed a unique identity incorporating spirituality, religion, language, laws, and community that shares similarities with First Nation and Europeans, but which at the same time is uniquely their own (Logan, 2015). They are, in other words, a hybrid of two nations. The Métis Nation is accurately described as a nation of its own. The Métis narrative is complex, inhabiting a space that is neither fully Indigenous nor fully white (Logan, 2015). These inconsistencies contribute to the invisible history of the Métis. That history is harder to grasp because there are few records of the relocations, removals, and dispersals suffered by the Métis people (Logan, 2015).

As a Métis woman in Canada, I feel I live between worlds, a member of Turtle Island and yet a **settler**. Many Indigenous people struggle with duality (Where do I fit as an Indigenous person? How do I remain Indigenous when oppression and government policy state otherwise?) (Lawrence, 2009). As a registered early childhood educator (RECE), someone who identifies as Métis, and someone who wanted to apply the TRC Calls to Action to my practice, I found that I needed to learn my traditions before I could implement culturally appropriate ECEC programming. This is the reality for many Indigenous people, as colonization has directly impacted our traditional ways of being (Lawrence, 2009).

## COLONIAL EDUCATION YESTERDAY AND TODAY

The Indian Act mandated that Indigenous children be educated at Indian residential schools (IRS) from 1883, with the last school closing in 1996 (Truth and Reconciliation Commission of Canada, 2015). The goal of IRS, as well as mainstream public schools, had been to assimilate Indigenous people into the dominant national culture (Putnam et al., 2011; Truth and Reconciliation Commission of Canada, 2015). Colonialism depends in part on the imposition of a standard of ideology against which others are measured and perceived to fail (Gupta, 2015). Mainstream public education, until very recently, has been devoid of Indigenous content, making the people and culture invisible (Putnam et al., 2011). The lack of curricular content further marginalizes an Indigenous population and deprives the non-Indigenous child of valuable information about the history, values, and ways of protecting resources of a culture that was here long before the prevailing society (Putnam et al., 2011).

In settler societies, inclusion and exclusion are set up to promote the settler as normative and superior and the Indigenous person as diverging and lesser (Bang et al., 2014). Official policies and regulations are based on these normative ideas, and educational facilities find their foundations in these practices (Bang et al., 2014). This approach forces Indigenous knowledge to conform to spaces defined by mainstream educational practices that support the settlers' normative world view (Putnam et al., 2011). Indigenous thought will not be successful in mainstream education if it is looked at as separate from or an add-on to the current curriculum.

Indigenous curriculum has the potential to transform the way we think; the challenge lies in whether or not we have the courage to step outside of our standardized classroom and embrace change (Zinga & Styres, 2011). In doing so, the colonial structure of education must allow for an embrace of the tangled power relations and endeavour to journey forward by creating ethical spaces where power relations are challenged in meaningful ways (Zinga & Styres, 2011). We can start by questioning our relationship with the land on which our institutions are located and by daring to question the historical and contemporary stories that are layered upon it.

In Canada, the K–12 curriculum is determined by each province or territory. As of 2020, in response to the TRC, some provinces and territories have begun to incorporate Indigenous knowledge and history in their curricula, while others have done nothing. For example, in British Columbia changes have been made in the K–12 curriculum and collaboration has occurred between provincial policy-makers and local Indigenous communities. School boards in the Yukon are starting to make similar changes, and they are using the BC curriculum as a model. In Manitoba, while teachers have access to various resources—for example, a 2003 resource on helping students understand Indigenous perspectives in the province and another on Indigenous language—these are not embedded within the Manitoba curriculum, and so remain merely optional. In Ontario, the social studies curriculum for grades 4 to 6, and the history curriculum for grades 7, 8, and 10, were updated with input from residential school survivors and other Indigenous partners. While Indigenous content in social studies for grades 1 to 3 and grade 9 geography were about to be updated in 2018, Ontario's newly elected Progressive Conservative government cancelled these changes. There is no mandatory Indigenous content in Quebec. In Nova Scotia, the provincial government and the Mi'kmaq in the province have worked together to create a document entitled *Treaty Education Framework for Curriculum Development.* Aimed at grades 1 to 12, local school boards have been working to integrate this content every year. But what about Indigenous education in the early years?

## EARLY CHILDHOOD EDUCATION PROGRAMS IN FIRST NATION AND INUIT COMMUNITIES

While there remains no national child-care program in Canada, the Canadian government began to fund Indigenous child care in 1994, initially through two programs: the First Nations and Inuit Child Care Initiative and the Aboriginal Head Start Initiative (Simon, 2018). The programs were offered in select urban areas and northern communities, with Aboriginal Head Start extended to on-reserve populations in 1998 (Prochner, 2004). These initiatives were conceptualized as early intervention programs to support culture, language, education, health, nutrition, communities, and parents, with Indigenous knowledge embedded in the curriculum (Greenwood, 2006; Prochner, 2004). Both curricula also embraced Indigenous pedagogy, allowing it to gain recognition and importance (Greenwood, 2006). Furthermore, as the initiatives were controlled by Indigenous peoples, this allowed for the full realization of culturally appropriate education (Greenwood, 2006). Researchers, with the support of Indigenous communities, demonstrated how this kind of investment in Indigenous early childhood programs resulted in positive outcomes that strengthened the community (Ball, 2005; Greenwood, 2006; Putnam et al., 2011; Somerville & Hickey, 2017).

Nevertheless, these early childhood programs, funded by the federal government and embraced by local Indigenous communities, still do not meet the full needs of the whole Indigenous population within Canada. According to Statistics Canada (2017), 867,415 Indigenous people lived in metropolitan areas in Canada in 2016. This accounts for over half of the country's Indigenous population. From 2006 to 2016, the number of Indigenous people living in a metropolitan area increased by 59.7 percent. From 2006 to 2016, the number of non-status Indians (as defined in the Indian Act) rose 75.1 percent, while the growth rate for status Indians was 30.8 percent. Non-status Indians account for nearly a quarter (232,375) of the First Nations population in Canada. Significantly, the Métis population also saw the fastest growth in Quebec (49.2 percent) and the Atlantic provinces (24.3 percent) (Statistics Canada, 2017).

The TRC's Call to Action for ECE programs was a restatement of the National Indian Brotherhood's 1972 policy paper, which called upon the Canadian government to support ECE programs within Indigenous communities (Simon, 2018). It stated, "unless a child learns about the forces which shape him, the history of his people, their values, their language, he will never really know himself or his potential as a human being" (National Indian Brotherhood, 1972, p. 9). In the 1990s, the First Nations and Inuit Child Care and Aboriginal Head Start

Initiatives were great starting points. Nonetheless, early childhood programs embedded in a few Indigenous communities across Canada only partly meet the National Indian Brotherhood's vision. There are Indigenous children throughout Canada, due to the restrictions of status (Indian Act) or their location, whether rural or urban, who still do not have access to culturally appropriate early childhood programs that embrace Indigenous knowledge.

## INDIGENOUS KNOWLEDGE

Traditional Indigenous knowledge can be defined as a way of life, an experiential relationship with family, spirits, animals, plants, and the land, an understanding and wisdom gained through generations of observation and teaching that uses indirect signals from nature or culture to predict future events or impacts (Ball, 2012; Emery, 2000; Ragoonaden & Mueller, 2017). It is based on the principles of relationships and balance (Townsend-Cross, 2004). Indigenous ways of knowing, being, and doing are based on the concept that everything and everyone is connected and balanced through relationships (Townsend-Cross, 2004). Indigenous knowledge is transmitted through holistic, reflective, experiential, and relational-focused connectedness (Ragoonaden & Mueller, 2017). Traditional knowledges are determined by the Indigenous communities, families, land, environments, and regions, and by the spiritual world, culture, and language (Ball, 2012). It is specific to a place and is rooted in the people.

The sharing of Indigenous knowledge has been introduced into some aspects of mainstream education. The challenge is to pose tough questions and push back on the margins and boundaries against labelling, stigmatizing, and the reinforcement of stereotypes (Tuck et al., 2014; Zinga & Styres, 2011). Mainstream educators and policy-makers often want to prescribe space for Indigenous content, usually a forest, which fits comfortably into their pedagogies and practice (Tuck et al., 2014; Zinga & Styres, 2011). But only when ancient teachings are rooted and old pedagogies embraced can a true understanding of self-in-relation occur. An Indigenous education is fundamentally based on a connection to the land and the holistic relationships that occur in a given space. It is based on a sense of place and the reciprocal relationship within that space (Ragoonaden & Mueller, 2017). Ultimately, it is the story of that space.

## LAND-BASED PEDAGOGY

Indigenous people understand land as an ancestral teacher, a holder of memory, and this relationship between people and land is familial, intimate, intergenerational, and instructive (Somerville & Hickey, 2017). Land can be defined as earth, water, and air. Land pedagogy is more than just the elements; it includes the spiritual, emotional, and intellectual aspects of the land. It is a living organism that exists in the past, present, and future (Styres et al., 2013).

There have been many initiatives incorporating land-based pedagogy rooted in Indigenous knowledge into elementary, secondary, and post-secondary curriculums (Bang et al., 2014; Somerville & Hickey, 2017; Styres et al., 2013; Tuck et al., 2014; Zinga & Styres, 2011). Each of these programs included a partnership between an Indigenous community, researchers, teachers, and students/children. The programs were rich in Indigenous knowledge of land, and the children participating in them benefitted.

### The Benefits of Land-Based Pedagogy

Somerville and Hickey (2017) describe a program in Sydney, Australia, in which elementary children, both Indigenous and non-Indigenous, were able to recapitalize their urban environment. The children learned about Indigenous language, plants, practices, and ways of being, which enabled them to "remake relations" within the urban landscape. The grade 8 children used art to represent the past, present, and future, thereby acknowledging the Indigenous past, the stark present, and the wonder and hope of the future. Space and time—past, present, and future—existed simultaneously. This idea of time and space coexisting also took root in Chicago with older secondary students (Bang et al.,

2014), and again in Toronto in the interaction with post-secondary students described by Styres et al. (2013). These elementary, secondary, and post-secondary students experienced land-based pedagogy by engaging in place stories that were rooted in Indigenous knowledge. They also interacted with the land through activities aimed at remembering childhood experiences that connected them to the land, re-examining the idea of land, and reconstructing old pedagogies that centred around land (Bang et al., 2014; Somerville & Hickey, 2017; Styres et al., 2013). The result is what Gupta (2015) describes as the pedagogy of "third space." The third space is where multiple realities interact. It is the grey area between diverse cultures and colonialism, a hybrid where two educational discourses are embedded into each other (Gupta, 2015). But although there is a richness to land-based programs and curriculums described in these studies, they are still working in isolation as mainstream public education systems and child-care centres fail to implement and engage in land-based pedagogies on a wider scale.

Indigenous knowledge and identity are based on relationships in which the past, present, and future are intertwined. It is within this space that our understandings of both Indigenous knowledge and identity will be called into question and reshaped. This is where the shift in how we—teachers, children, and communities—relate to the world. The decision to think critically and notice is a pedagogical act that will impact ways of being. The TRC's Calls to Action have started the shift toward a space in which Indigenous knowledge and identity can be (re)claimed.

## MAKING SPACE FOR INDIGENOUS KNOWLEDGE IN AN URBAN CHILD-CARE CENTRE

As a member of the Anishinaabe, Chippewa Nation, and Métis, I wondered what this space could look like and the influence it would have on an urban child-care community. I wondered how a colonial institution, in this case an early childhood centre, might make space physically, spiritually, and psychologically for Indigenous knowledge. How would creating space based on the Indigenous concept of relationality affect the way teachers, children, and families gathered? Indigenous relationality can be defined as social, moral, spiritual, and community obligations that help provide an ordered universe in which humans, animals, plants, and the elements are in balance (Graham, 2014). The attributes of relationality are empathy (ethics), identity (place), autonomy, and balance (Graham, 2014). Relationality is realized through stewardship and a cultivation of a sense of being, belonging, and connectedness.

I wanted to know whether a community's engagement with relationality would allow it to embrace multiple ways of knowing and being. The approach I took in this project can be described as action research, a cyclical process aimed at improving practice (MacNaughton & Hughes, 2009; Mukerji & Albon, 2015). The research was conducted during the early fall in a preschool room with children between the ages of two and a half and four. Because I worked as an RECE in that room, I took on the role of teacher-researcher. Fourteen children and seven educators participated in the project. They were recruited through a letter and information session. The letter was taped to the child's cubby for their parents/guardians, and the parents/guardians were then invited to an information session, with a poster on the classroom door serving as a reminder of the date and time. The recruitment of children continued throughout the fall as families entered the program. The RECEs were recruited through a letter placed in their mailboxes, and a separate information session was offered to them. A consent form was presented at the information sessions, and these were also placed in the common area of the centre's front lobby for one week. Those who wished to participate were asked to submit their consent form in a box. A verbal script was presented to the children during the information session with their parents, for their informed consent, and verbal consent was sought from the children throughout the research.

Data collection occurred over a two-month period in which emergent learning opportunities were documented. Learning opportunities occur naturally, spontaneously, and daily within the curriculum, and it is the role and responsibility of the educator to offer guidance and facilitation. The learning opportunities documented in this study were based on Indigenous pedagogy that had been occurring in the classroom. I was interested primarily in undertaking an examination of the interactions and pedagogies that were thriving in this learning space.

It is worth noting that pedagogical documentation is a part of RECEs' daily roles and responsibilities in Ontario. The Ontario Ministry of Education's main pedagogical document for early years education, *How Does Learning Happen?*, describes this documentation as "more than recording events—it is a means to learning about how children think and learn" (Ontario Ministry of Education, 2014, p. 21); it further defines pedagogical documentation as "a way to make children's learning and understanding of the world around them visible" (p. 21).

I used field notes, photographs, videos, and audio recordings to generate pedagogical documentation. In my field notes I recorded significant events that were observed. They also included my feelings, reactions, and personal reflections and analyses (Mukherji & Albon, 2015; Patton, 2015). In this action research, field notes were used to gain a greater insight into how Indigenous knowledge is affecting individuals, and into the space involved in the study. The field notes supported the examination of my own professional practice. The use of visual and audio media also supported the action research by helping me gain an in-depth understanding of the situation. They enhanced data collection by capturing details my observations and field notes may have missed.

Additionally, a focus group of RECEs who worked in the preschool room met twice for an open discussion on Indigenous pedagogy and to reflect on the experiences offered to the children. A focus group allows the researcher to interview a small group of people on a specific topic, with the goal being "to get high-quality data in a social context where people can consider their own views in the context of the views of others" (Patton, 2015, p. 386). A focus group captures subjective comments with the intent of evaluating them to gain an understanding of perceptions, feelings, attitudes, and motivations (Edmunds, 2000).

In sum, a large quantity of information was gathered through field notes, observations, video and audio recordings, reflective journalling, photographs, artifacts, and focus groups. In total, there were 5 video recordings, 2 audio recordings, 1 field notebook, 1 reflective journal,

20 artifacts, 600 photographs, 2 transcribed focus group sessions, and numerous daily observations. The information was processed through thematic analysis. The data was initially coded into 15 categories, with 4 major themes emerging.

### Aabawaadiziwin

September is the month of new beginnings at the child-care centre. A group of new preschool-age children enroll in the program. Typically, it is their first time away from their parents. The transition to the program can be a time of heightened emotion. This was the case for one boy. He sat at his cubby crying and speaking Mandarin. His eyes darted around the room; his facial expressions conveyed his uncertainty about the environment. My heart was full of empathy; I sat near him while respecting his personal space. As I sat there, I observed a small yellow bird outside in the garden. It had landed on the head of a pink corn-flower. It was beautiful. I pointed toward the window to the bird. The boy followed my hand and noticed the tiny yellow bird balancing on the flower. He moved closer to me with curiosity. I said softly, "bird." He crossed the room to the window, motioning for me to follow. Together, we watched this beautiful, pale yellow bird perched on the small pink flower. Time stood still for a moment. The flower gently swayed back and forth in the wind. The boy looked at me with a smile, then flapped his arms and said something in Mandarin. I flapped my arms and said, "bird." We smiled at each other and continued to watch the bird. When the bird flew away, the child began to play comfortably in the classroom. From that point on, he was excited to be at school. He would enter the room with a smile and seek me out.

This event helped me and the child begin building a relationship; it was a magical moment that we shared together. I used my relation-ship with the land, animals, and plants to help bridge the gap between the two of us. As I reflect back, I wonder if the bird purposely came by to support our relationship. In the moment, the land, which includes the animals and plants, offered us the opportunity for a universal lan-guage. The boy and I were able to find a common language and a ground, physically and metaphorically, on which to develop a secure relationship.

*Aabawaadiziwin* is the Anishinaabek word meaning togetherness, the act of being together (Simpson, 2011). It means we must practise good relationships with all living beings around us. The land helps us practise good relationships. In this instant, it offered a moment in which the boy and I could together witness life in its purest.

Another educator also experienced a moment of *aabawaadiziwin* while attending a water blessing walk. She shared with me how during the walk her heart was overflowing with gratitude toward the water and land. This experience helped her to realize the extent to which the land, including the water, gives of itself to animals and to us humans. She experienced the realization that we are all connected to the land. During the walk, she also observed how the children interacted with the land; they were slowing down, looking closely, and setting forth with purpose. The educator became profoundly aware of relationships between the children and the adults. The land strengthened the bond between the two. She was overwhelmed with the beauty of watching the children and adults interact with and through the land. The experience impacted her practice. She began the process of reflecting on how best to implement this strong connection to the land on a daily basis within an urban community. The water blessing walk allowed her to experience a fundamental connection to the land and the holistic relationships that occur in a given space. She experienced what Ragoonaden and Mueller (2017) describe as a sense of place and the reciprocal relationship with that space while practising Indigenous knowledge. The educator's reflection of the walk captures how land pedagogy is more than the elements—it is spiritual, emotional, and intellectual (Styres et al., 2013).

## Dawaa

The playground outside the classroom is large. For some children, this is what they need to start feeling a sense of belonging; it allows them to run and explore the area. For other children, the physical space is too large. Their body language indicates an uneasiness; they linger near the edges of the yard and by the doors. I decided to approach these children individually with scissors and a basket. I asked for help harvesting the cedar tree. A group of children followed me. As I approached the tree, I said its name, "cedar." I greeted it with a small shake. I rubbed my hands on the branches and let the fragrance cover my hand. The smell engulfed the children. I repeated the name, "cedar." Out loud I stated my intention to the tree, asking for permission to harvest some branches. Peggy Pitwanakwat, from the First Peoples at Seneca, taught me this traditional practice. In my heart I felt warmth and an acceptance of my request, and I offered water to the plant as thanks. Typically, tobacco is offered; however, when that is not available, water is substituted. I cut a few branches. The children watched, and I encouraged them to follow. One child grabbed a branch and looked for approval. I nodded my head. He cut and the other children followed.

We filled the basket. More children gathered around us. We moved to a large, flat stump nearby. The children cut the cedar into tiny pieces. The smell of cedar filled the air. I talked about how we could make tea with the cedar. A child left and reappeared with a container of water. A tea party commenced. A small group of children continued to cut the cedar and place it on my head as a "crown." The tea party continued, with everyone wearing crowns of cedar. The cedar fragrance engulfed the air. Some of the children, who were emotional (crying, upset, sad) at the beginning of the outside play, were by the end calm, smiling, and laughing.

*Giizhik*, cedar, is a traditional Indigenous medicine. It is often used in smudging. It is the medicine of protection. Cedar is an old, wise, and powerful spirit. The smell of cedar is comforting and protective. It is often used to cleanse a new house, inviting unwanted energies to leave peacefully. Did using this medicine help the children feel safe? There was a sense of calmness after this activity. The children seemed willing to engage in their new surroundings.

A portion of the *giizhik* gathered was used in smudging. Smudging was introduced at a group meeting a few days later. I showed the children three of the sacred medicines, white sage, sweetgrass, and cedar. I passed the medicine around the group. The children smelled each medicine; they particularly liked the sweetgrass. I spoke about how sweetgrass has a sweet aroma; it reminds people of gentleness, love, and kindness. I explained how we hold a piece of the medicine in our hands and think about good intentions. Then it is placed in a shell and lit with fire. The smoke is brought to our heads to think good thoughts, to our eyes to see good things, to our ears to hear good words, to our mouth to speak goodness, then finally to our hearts to feel good. I showed them how to smudge. They copied my gestures. Thereafter the children asked that group meetings begin with smudging. Each day good intentions are smudged, filling the room with the smell of cedar, sage, and sweetgrass.

A teacher shared with me how a group of children were helping her prepare the garden for the winter. She thought it would be appropriate to do a smudging to offer the earth good intentions for its winter sleep. Each child held a piece of sage and placed it in the shell. As the teacher burnt the medicine, a child said, "Now, the goodness is everywhere."

One morning, after a parent observed the children smudging, she related to me how in her culture they have something similar. They burn a plant to purify the energy in a space. As we spoke about our smudging rituals, and other traditions, we realized how much we had in common. Our hearts were filled with warmth for the similarities of humanity.

*Dawaa* translates into space, a gap, room. These are examples of how we were able to co-create a space based on the Indigenous concept of relationality. I was able to use the Indigenous practice of harvesting to help the new children to transition into a new environment. Smudging became a natural part of our daily practice. Another educator transferred this practice into her teaching approach, resulting in a beautiful moment with a child. The conversation between me and the parent connected two different cultures based on their similarities. *Dawaa* for Indigenous knowledge was co-constructed. Indigenous knowledge is based on the concept that everything and everyone is connected and balanced through relationships (Townsend-Cross, 2004). The relationship between educator, children, and parent was being strengthened through the power of Indigenous ways and practices.

### Biiwide

As noted earlier, two focus group sessions were conducted, one near the beginning of the research, with six participants, and the final one at the end, with four educators. A theme that appeared throughout the first session was the idea of not knowing, whether that took the form of "I know nothing about Indigenous People" or "I was not taught in school." This produced a sense of not knowing how to teach or what to teach in regard to Indigenous knowledge. Over half of the educators expressed a fear of "doing it wrong." Sarah Dion (2007) describes this phenomenon as the "perfect stranger." The fear of offending limits the educator to their current practices. The perfect stranger also unconsciously silences the need to question teaching ways that challenge the dominant story of Canada. In general, the lack of knowledge about Canada's relationship and history with Indigenous Peoples is continued through the perfect stranger (*biiwide* means "stranger"). The majority of the educators were unaware of prior research about Indigenous practices and pedagogy. Through their involvement in the research, the educators began a new dialogue that investigated their relationship with Indigenous knowledge, practices, and ways. The members of the second focus group expressed that they found the experience rewarding. This new knowledge deepened their understanding of their relationship with the land. A true connection to space or place occurred naturally through the process. The educators expressed that they approached land and children differently. Their thinking had shifted. They felt a desire to act on their informed teaching approach and to continue to learn and unlearn certain practices and ways of being.

### Biskaabiiyang

The participants in the focus groups spoke of their deep appreciation of my willingness to share and educate them on Indigenous knowledge, ways, and practices. I struggled with this notion. As part of a minority population, whom the Canadian government and society continues to neglect and oppress, why must I educate the oppressors? Why is it my responsibility to educate the dominant society on how not to oppress?

I spent quite a bit of time reflecting on the matter. What is my role, my responsibility to my ancestors, my future grandchildren, and to my present? How do I reconcile the pain? How do I decolonize? How do I, Chippewa and Métis, walk the path between the dominant society and my Indigenous identity?

I smudged, I embraced my Anishinaabe traditions, I retold my story to myself, I read, I asked for guidance from my ancestors, and I reflected. I struggled. I reflected some more. Unknowingly, I was engaged in *Biskaabiiyang*. Leanne Simpson references this term in her book *Dancing on Our Turtle's Back* and includes a definition of it by the Anishinaabe scholar Wendy Makoon Genusz, who describes it as

> a process through which Anishinaabe researchers evaluate how they personally have been affected by colonization, rid themselves of the emotional and psychological baggage they carry from this process, and then return to their ancestral traditions.... When using Biskaabiiyang methodologies, an individual must recognize and deal with this negative kind of thinking.... This is the only way to conduct new research that will be beneficial to the continuation of anishnaabe-gikendasssowin (knowledge, information, and the synthesis of personal teachings). (as cited in Simpson, 2011, p. 50)

After much reflection, there came a point where all I could feel was *zaagi'idiwin*—love.

In Anishinaabe communities there are seven teachings called the Grandfather Teachings. These teachings help the Anishinaabe people walk in harmony on the earth. They help build relationships within a community. Love is one of the teachings. The Grandfathers describe love as the ability to draw from the heart when we relate to others. When a preschooler was asked, "What is love?" she put her hands to her chest and said, "It's my heart." In the simplest action and words, she reminded me of the true essence of the teaching, to act from the heart. Love is the capacity for kindness and caring. What if I relate and lead with love? This concept shifted my paradigm. Love is filled with truth, another Grandfather teaching. *Debwewin*, truth, is spoken from the heart. It means to be true to all things, to yourself, and to your place in life. Truth is learning by living and speaking it. My truth and place in life is as an educator.

As an early childhood educator, I practise *zhinoomoowin*, the art of showing someone something, to act or to show how it is done, or modelling desirable behaviours (Simpson, 2011). I had been using *zhinoomoowin* throughout this research with children and my colleagues to positive effect. The educators participating in the research have started the decolonization dialogue and embraced Indigenous knowledge, practices, and ways into their daily work because of *zhinoomoowin*. I have been their guide in the process of reconciliation and resurgence.

I have walked the good path with children for a very long time, helping and guiding them along the way. It is time for me to intentionally walk the good path with educators. By leading with love and speaking truths, maybe we can co-construct a new story, a new space in which the Indigenous idea of relationality, being in balance through relationships with everything and everyone, is our guiding light.

## RECOMMENDATIONS

This research shows it is possible to make space for Indigenous knowledge within an urban preschool room. The process of decolonizing teaching approaches requires dialogue between settler and Indigenous educators. To truly achieve the Calls to Action set forth by the TRC for culturally appropriate early childhood programs in Ontario would require the support of the Ontario Ministry of Education. The Ministry of Education is the regulating body for licensed child-care and early years programs within the province (Ontario Ministry of Education, 2018). The Child Care and Early Years Act of 2014 is the legislation that governs the standards child-care and early year programs must achieve to receive and renew their licences (Ontario Ministry of Education, 2018). Subsection 55 (3) authorizes the Ministry of Education to issue policy statements about programming and pedagogy for the purpose of guiding operators of child-care and early year programs in developing their programs and services (Ontario

Ministry of Education, 2018). The Ministry of Education currently guides licensed child-care programs using the pedagogy document *How Does Learning Happen? Ontario's Pedagogy for the Early Years* (Ontario Ministry of Education, 2018). An amendment to the legislation is recommended to support the process of reconciliation. The amendment would require child-care centres to employ an Indigenous pedagogist to support the implementation of Indigenous knowledge. Adding sections on land-based pedagogy to *How Does Learning Happen?* would support centres in developing new practices that are influenced by Indigenous knowledge.

In addition, it is recommended that ECEC pre-service programs offer courses on Indigenous knowledge and pedagogy. Early childhood programs are ideal starting points to instill awareness of Indigenous knowledge and pedagogy. A positive transformation based on reconciliation and resurgence could occur in the field through the education of future early childhood educators.

## CRITICAL THINKING QUESTIONS

1. Does your pre-service early learning program incorporate Indigenous learnings and practices? If not, why do you think this is the case?
2. What are the benefits of Indigenous ways of knowing for all children in all ECEC programs?
3. Have you read the TRC report? Or the 94 Calls to Action?
4. What actions will you take?
5. What does your province need to do?

## GLOSSARY OF KEY TERMS

**culturally appropriate early childhood education programs:** In the context of the TRC, ECE programs in Indigenous communities— be they First Nations, Inuit, or Métis—that are led by Indigenous people. Such programs recognize the importance of Indigenous cultures, languages, and knowledges, and the right to self-determination.

**Indian Act:** A federal law that governs matters connected to Indian status, bands, and reserves. It has played a fundamental role in the oppression and domination of the Indigenous Peoples in Canada.

**settler:** A person who comes from elsewhere and either participates in the colonization of the land or benefits from the fact the land has been colonized.

## REFERENCES

Ball, J. (2005). Early childhood care and development programs as hook and hub for inter-sectoral service delivery in First Nations communities. *Journal of Aboriginal Health, 2*(1), 36–50.

Ball, J. (2012). Identity and knowledge in Indigenous young children's experiences in Canada. *Childhood Education, 88*(5), 286–291.

Bang, M., Curley, L., Kessel, A., Marin, A., Suzukovich III, E., & Strack, G. (2014). Muskrat theories, tobacco in the streets, and living in Chicago as Indigenous land. *Environmental Education Research, 20*(1), 37–55.

Dion, S. D. (2007). Disrupting molded images: Identities, responsibilities and relationships—Teachers and indigenous subject material. *Teaching Education, 18*(4), 329–342.

Edmunds, H. (2000). *The focus group research handbook.* McGraw-Hill.

Emery, A. (2000). *Integrating Indigenous knowledge in project planning and implementation.* World Bank.

Graham, M. (2014). Aboriginal notions of relationality and positionalism: A reply to Weber. *Global Discourse, 4*(1), 17–22.

Greenwood, M. (2006). Children are a gift to us: Aboriginal-specific early childhood programs and services in Canada. *Canadian Journal of Native Education, 29*(1), 12–28.

Gupta, A. (2015). Pedagogy of third space: A multidimensional early childhood curriculum. *Policy Futures in Education, 13*(2), 260–272.

Lawrence, B. (2003). Gender, race, and the regulations of Native identity in Canada and the United States: An overview. *Hypatia, 18*(2), 3–31.

Lawrence, B. (2009). *"Real" Indians and others: Mixed-blood urban Native peoples and Indigenous nationhood.* Point Par Point.

Logan, T. (2015). Settler colonialism in Canada and the Métis. *Journal of Genocide Research, 17*(4), 433–452.

MacNaughton, G., & Hughes, P. (2009). *Doing action research in early childhood studies.* Open University Press.

Mukherji, P., & Albon, D. (2015). *Research methods in early childhood* (2nd ed.). SAGE Publications.

National Indian Brotherhood. (1972). *Indian control of Indian education.* National Indian Brotherhood.

Ontario Ministry of Education. (2014). *How does learning happen? Ontario's pedagogy for the early years.* Ontario Ministry of Education. http://www.edu.gov.on.ca/childcare/HowLearningHappens.pdf

Ontario Ministry of Education. (2018). *Child care licensing.* Service Ontario. http://www.edu.gov.on.ca/childcare/

Patton, M. (2015). *Qualitative research and evaluation methods* (4th ed.). SAGE Publications.

Prochner, L. (2004). Early childhood education programs for Indigenous children in Canada, Australia and New Zealand: An historical review. *Australian Journal of Early Childhood, 29*(4), 7–16.

Putnam, J. W., Putnam, D., Jerome, B., & Jerome, R. (2011). Cross-cultural collaboration for locally developed Indigenous curriculum. *International Journal of Multicultural Education, 13*(2), 1–18.

Ragoonaden, K., & Mueller, L. (2017). Culturally responsive pedagogy: Indigenizing curriculum. *Canadian Journal of Higher Education, 47*(2), 22–46.

Royal Commission on Aboriginal Peoples. (1996). *Report of the Royal Commission on Aboriginal Peoples: Vol. 3. Gathering strength.* Canadian Government Publishing, Public Works and Government Services.

Simon, M. (2017). *An ecological mode approach to Indigenous identity* [Unpublished manuscript]. Seneca College, School of Early Childhood Education.

Simon, M. (2018). *Honouring the Truth and Reconciliation Commission* [Unpublished manuscript]. Seneca College, School of Early Childhood Education.

Simpson, L. (2011). *Dancing on our turtle's back: Stories of Nishnaabeg re-creation, resurgence and a new emergence.* Arbeiter Ring Publishing.

Somerville, M., & Hickey, S. (2017). Between Indigenous and non-Indigenous: Urban/nature/child pedagogies. *Environmental Education Research, 23*(10), 1427–1439.

Statistics Canada. (2017, October 25). *2016 census topic: Aboriginal peoples.* https://
www12.statcan.gc.ca/census-recensement/2016/rt-td/ap-pa-eng.cfm

Styres, S., Haig-Brown, C., & Blimkie, M. (2013). Towards a pedagogy of land: The
urban context. *Canadian Journal of Education, 36*(2), 34–67.

Townsend-Cross, M. (2004). Indigenous Australian perspectives in early childhood
education. *Australian Journal of Early Childhood, 29*(4), 1–6.

Truth and Reconciliation Commission of Canada. (2015). *Honouring the truth,
reconciling for the future.* Truth and Reconciliation Commission of Canada.

Tuck, E., McKenzie, M., & McCoy, K. (2014). Land education: Indigenous,
post-colonial and decolonizing perspectives on place and environmental
education research. *Environmental Education Research, 20*(1), 1–23.

Zinga, D., & Styres, S. (2011). Pedagogy of land: Tensions, challenges, and
contradictions. *First Nations Perspectives, 4,* 59–83.

# CHAPTER 8

# Failure and Loss as a Methodological, Relational, and Ethical Necessity in Teaching and Learning in the Early Years

*Maria Karmiris*

## LEARNING OBJECTIVES

- To discuss and identify the limits of child developmentalism as a hegemonic practice and discourse in ECE
- To consider the negative impacts experienced by children through the implementation of child development theories and practices
- To engage in the application of other critical discourses such as disability studies in order to pursue the aims and objectives of equity as praxis

## INTRODUCTION

According to post-structural feminist scholar Donna Haraway (2016), "bounded individualism in its many flavours in science, politics, and philosophy has finally become unavailable to think with, truly no longer thinkable, technically or any other way" (p. 5). Haraway's reference to the unthinkability of bounded individualism offers a stark critique of the conception of the human through the age of the so-called

Enlightenment. I also read her provocative critique of the neoliberal subject as a call to early childhood educators to accept the ultimate failure and loss of orientations toward the current normative order. In considering the **normative neoliberal subject** as a failed and failing story, it is important to recognize and confront that its failure is routed/rooted through its paradoxical insistence on its own hegemony. Even as the conception of the normative neoliberal subject daily fails children and youth within the education system, it remains fiercely resilient and insistent that this pathway is the best and only pathway forward. Thus, one of the aims of this chapter is to confront the ways in which discourses of child development continue to sustain the current neoliberal order and its adherences to normalcy.

In this chapter, the use of the term *normative neoliberal subject* follows the work of numerous scholars who point to the ways the Western, heteronormative, white, male, able-bodied, middle-class subject remains the standard measure of how gradations of the human come to be counted as human (Baker, 2015; Erevelles, 2000, 2005, 2018; MacLure et al., 2010; Michalko, 2002; Mitchell et al., 2014; Slee, 2019; Stephens & Cryle, 2017). I wonder here about how the discourses of child development remain taken for granted in ways that sustain the conditions of exclusion through explicit and implicit manifestations of racism, classism, ableism, sexism, and homophobia. I wonder, too, how training and expecting early childhood educators to monitor and observe children based on the successful achievement of particular developmental milestones simultaneously sets up the conditions to read racialized, classed, gendered, and disabled children as always and already failing to measure up.

This chapter is composed of two parts. The first part considers the resiliency and subsequent consequences of sustaining the failing story of the normative neoliberal subject within early childhood education. This occurs through a critique of developmentalism as a prominent feature that guides the observation, assessment, and evaluation of children. The second part considers what happens when early childhood educators refuse and resist the assumption that the principles of child developmentalism remain central to evaluating, teaching, and learning practices and instead foreground teaching and learning as a relational engagement among a myriad of embodied racialized, gendered, classed, and disabled differences.

I will explore how the intersections of the fields of **disability studies**, post-colonial studies, and decolonial and post-structural feminisms can inhabit the failure and loss of the current normative order as a mechanism to imagine and enact distinctly different teaching and learning possibilities.

Ultimately, this chapter aims to contribute to the vibrant work of re-imagining teaching and learning by engaging in equity as a deeply embedded praxis (see chapter 3; Abawi & Berman, 2019; MacNevin & Berman, 2017; Portelli & Eizadirad, 2018).

## CONFRONTING THE FAILED AND FAILING MYTH OF CHILD DEVELOPMENT

The ubiquity of required courses on child and human development in early childhood education (ECE) programs, as well as in programs of elementary teacher education, across Canada is not only undeniable but remains taken for granted as integral to adhering to and sustaining current curricular orientations in both early years and school settings. More specifically, courses in ECE programs that espouse the work of theorists like Piaget and Erikson, such as human development and child development, are assumed to be necessary foundations. The aim of such courses is to train and thus sustain orientations toward observing how our youngest learners meet, exceed, and/or fail to measure up to developmental milestones. Several scholars who have focused on a critical analysis of the history of modern schooling have outlined their concerns about the tangible impacts in the everyday lives of young children who are labelled as not measuring up to "normative standards" (Baker, 2015; Ellis, 2019; Farley, 2018; McGuire, 2017; Stephens & Cryle, 2017; Walkerdine, 1993). Implicit in the act of observing and monitoring through any number of checklists and criteria that link milestones, such as sitting, walking, talking, and self-feeding, to age-appropriate development are the subsequent relationships to mechanisms of diagnosis, categorization, and pathologization (Baker, 2015; Ellis, 2019; Farley, 2018; McGuire, 2017; Stephens & Cryle, 2017; Walkerdine, 1993). It is the inextricable linkages between orientations of educator observation, current conceptions of childhood development, and practices of diagnosing children who do not measure up as problematic that must be confronted, troubled, and disrupted in ECE policies and practices.

As a practising elementary school teacher steeped in the discourses and practices of childhood development since 2002, I apply my own method of confronting and troubling these discourses. I seek to address the fundamental ethical dilemma of being mired in what Indigenous scholar and researcher Eve Tuck (2009) refers to as "the binary of reproduction and resistance" (p. 419). Tuck emphasizes the ways cycles of resistance enact cycles of hegemonic reformation of colonial Western logics. In our contemporary moment of reformation, colonial Western logics are also referred to as the normative neoliberal order. These cycles of reform are particularly evident in the field of education, where despite decades of critique and calls for reform, schools continue to engage in sorting, categorizing, and conditionally including students. A component part of confronting and refusing to participate in the cycles of reform that sustain the hegemony of the normative neoliberal subject is accepting the inextricable linkages between Western modernity, coloniality, and injustice. Mignolo's (2011) work serves as a reminder that "coloniality is constitutive of modernity—there is no modernity without coloniality" (p. 3). Put differently, the social injustice, marginalization, exploitation, and oppression of coloniality are necessary for the functioning of Western modernity. Thus, in sustaining the hegemony of the normative neoliberal subject, there must also be the recognition within ECE that there is a simultaneous sustenance of the colonial legacies of injustice. Those of us who teach and learn with young children must address their own feelings of provocation vis-à-vis critical scholars like Haraway (2016), Tuck (2009), and Mignolo (2011).

In order to do this, I turn to the work of scholars who have studied the history of education and its subsequent exclusions based on the criteria of who counts as normal. I also connect this scholarship to an example from my own teaching practice to demonstrate the ways the resiliency of the neoliberal subject is dependent upon the act of reproducing the conditions for failure and exclusion. Walkerdine (1993), a critical psychologist, drawing on the work of Foucault, offered a scathing critique of developmentalism that remains as relevant today as it was nearly thirty years ago:

> The very idea of development is not natural and universal but extremely specific and, in its specificity, occludes other marginalized stories, subsumed as they are within a bigger story. The big story is a European patriarchal story, a story from the centre which describes the periphery in terms of the abnormal, difference as deficiency. (p. 455)

I quote Walkerdine (1993) to show that my concerns with discourses of child development are neither new nor unique. Rather, my concerns are situated within countless decades of resistance to a Eurocentric conception of child development that remains central to contemporary teaching and learning practices. How does ECE, through its adherence to discourses and practices of child development, remain complicit in the resiliency of the neoliberal normative order and its injustices? I contend that finding ways to avoid reproducing the conditions of injustice by refusing to sustain the hegemony of the normative neoliberal subject remains the most pressing ethical dilemma education must confront.

Contemporary scholarship in the field of education not only substantiates Walkerdine's (1993) critique of discourses and practices in child development as "necessary to construct a knowledge of a population to be governed" (p. 453), but also points with significant urgency at the need to stop the mechanisms of reproduction of the normative neoliberal subject. For example, it is impossible to read Ellis's (2019) work tracing the evolution of segregated special needs and English-language-learner classes over the last century of modern schooling in Toronto without attending to the ways Eurocentric conceptions of child and human development continue to remain both resilient and hegemonic. Concerns related to the mental hygiene of young children a century ago (Ellis, 2019) are now encapsulated under the terms *mental health and well-being* and/or *self-regulation*. Debates between the false binary of nature (eugenicists) and nurture (environmentalists) a century ago (Ellis, 2019) continue in this very moment as disability consistently provides a rationale for exclusion (Erevelles, 2018; McGuire, 2017; Slee, 2019). Ellis (2019) offers a quote from Angus McLaren, a well-known eugenicist in the early twentieth century, who said, "It is important not to exaggerate the gap that separated the eugenicists from the environmentalists. Although their methods differed, their goals of efficient social management were similar" (p. 185). In other words, while there have been numerous debates over the course of modern schooling as conceptualized in the global North, in relation to which version of Eurocentric child development might take the foreground for a given period of time, these seeming tensions have only succeeded in reproducing a continued adherence to the neoliberal normative order. The same normative practices and logic have been repackaged using different terminology with the same hierarchical power relations.

As Walkerdine (1993) notes, "the big story is a European patriarchal story, a story from the centre which describes the periphery in terms of the abnormal, difference as deficiency" (p. 455). Within this story, the failed and failing myth of childhood development, and all educators who are embedded in it, invariably and disproportionally observe Black, disabled, immigrant, and/or socio-economically disadvantaged children as failed and failing. There are so many qualitative and quantitative research studies that make this point that it seems redundant and excessive to list them here. However, I do want to contribute an example from my own teaching and learning experiences with "Vinisha" (as I'll call her) as a way to consider the tangible impacts of continuing to sustain the hegemony of the normative neoliberal subject.

Vinisha, who identified as Jamaican-Canadian with a diagnosed learning disability, arrived in my class in the middle of the school year. Before I even met her, I was told by my principal that Vinisha was trouble. Indeed, she was being transferred from a neighbouring school due to numerous suspensions and persistent challenges in meeting classroom learning goals. Before I even met her, her Ontario

Student Record (OSR) arrived. Her OSR was full of reports and assessments from psychologists, social workers, and occupational therapists who documented all the ways this child did not measure up to the developmentally appropriate standards for her age. These documents told a story of a consistent failure to meet normative standards, from Vinisha's kindergarten year through to her early years of elementary school. Read as failed and failing by a network of educators, psychologists, and social workers, I was invited to read her through the same onto-epistemological orientations.

It is important to stop here and consider the implications of sustaining rather than questioning and disrupting readings of students like Vinisha as failures before even engaging in any tangible encounters to teach and learn with each other. In sustaining the hegemony of the normative neoliberal subject, Vinisha is always and already read as a failure before she has exchanged her first hellos with me or any other educator. Invariably this sustains a power imbalance between teacher and student whereby the teacher is read as the solver of the problem that Vinisha poses to the normative order. In this reading, Vinisha must be scrutinized, monitored, excessively observed, and evaluated. In the context of hierarchical power relations, strategies must be implemented, documented, and repeatedly re-evaluated in order to ensure that all necessary measures are applied so that her failure to measure up addresses the need to strive for normative developmental milestones. In this reading, normative developmental milestones are never questioned as inappropriate and ineffective mechanisms within which Vinisha is situated and against which she is measured. Rather, in this reading of Vinisha as always and already a failure, the hegemony of the normative neoliberal subject is sustained at great cost to the possibilities of teaching and learning differently with Vinisha and her classmates.

The unfortunate reality for countless students like Vinisha is that these sorts of readings remain so ubiquitous and commonplace that they continue to have a tangibly negative impact on these students' experiences within school. Thus, in order to engage in equity as a praxis we must not only disrupt, resist, and question such readings—we must also look to transform our reading of students like Vinisha. According to Haraway

(2016), "staying with the trouble requires making odd kin; that is, we require each other in unexpected collaborations and combinations.... We become with each other or not at all" (p. 4). What Haraway (2016) suggests here as a response to the ways "bounded individualism has become unavailable to think with" (p. 5) is the necessity of finding different ways to reach toward each other so as to re-imagine the possibilities of our interdependence. I take this call to early childhood educators as an encouragement to not only stop reading, repeating, and sustaining stories of students as failing to measure up to normative standards, but also to disrupt conceptions of what it means to fail.

What happens when we begin to reorient our conceptions of what it means to fail? What happens when failing is read as something good, productive, and indeed necessary (Halberstam, 2011; Mitchell et al., 2014)? Considering ways Vinisha might thrive in school reorients failure as representative of structural barriers steeped in ableism, racism, classism, and hetero-patriarchy, and not of individual deficits or deficiencies. Rather than remaining anchored in the discourses, policies, and practices of child developmentalism, with their focus on monitoring individuals, I follow Haraway's (2016) provocation to make "odd kin" (p. 4). Similarly, I invite early childhood educators to engage in new and innovative collaborations through critical scholarship and research occurring across disability studies, post-colonial studies, decolonial studies, and post-structural feminisms (Erevelles, 2018; Haraway, 2016; Pacini-Ketchabaw, 2012; Slee, 2019; Tuck, 2009). Through these collaborations we might disrupt the ways the neoliberal normative order persistently re-establishes its hegemony. We might also begin to read failure through its productive possibilities (Halberstam, 2011; Mitchell et al., 2014). In other words, what happens when "failing normalization practices" (Mitchell et al., 2014, pp. 299–300) are read as invitational opportunities to re-imagine our teaching and learning relationships? Within this context, teaching and learning with Vinisha is no longer reduced to measuring her adherence to the milestones of the normative neoliberal subject. Rather, Vinisha and her numerous encounters with fellow students and teachers can be read as opportunities to learn from and with a network of complex interactions with varying and diverse embodied differences.

The call for this kind of transformation and reorientation is necessary since the hegemony of the current normative neoliberal order depends on sustaining the conditions of failure for countless students. In this way, as suggested by the provocations from Haraway (2016), Halberstam (2011), and Mitchell et al. (2014), failure becomes the opportunity to rewrite the script so that Vinisha can be read with and through the fruitful contributions she can make within her learning community. In their advocacy for enacting substantive practices toward the inclusion of disabled students, Mitchell et al. (2014) describe what happens when "what appears on the surface as disabled students' incapacity to keep up with their normative peers turns out to be a purposeful failure.… Within the multiplying paradoxes of neoliberal inclusionism, crip success is, paradoxically the failure to become normate" (p. 300). Their work allows educators to consider failure to meet the normative neoliberal subject as good and necessary. Vinisha's failure can be read as good trouble, the kind of trouble that offers opportunities to ask important questions about the kinds of assessment and evaluation practices teachers engage in daily. If the measure of success is sustained by the normative neoliberal subject, then failure is not only necessary, but also important in creating conditions in which students like Vinisha can teach us how to learn differently with each other.

Thus far, I have outlined the fundamental dilemmas resulting from sustaining the kinds of policies and practices that adhere to measuring and observing students based on the discourses of childhood developmentalism. The pervasive and ubiquitous presence of these practices within ECE continues to sustain the hegemony of the normative neoliberal subject. I have also explored the ways discourses of failure are inextricably linked to maintaining and sustaining the hegemony of the normative neoliberal subject through current evaluation practices. Discourses of failure invariably expose the racism, classism, ableism, and hetero-patriarchy that the neoliberal order depends on for its survival. In his call for decoloniality, Mignolo (2011) contends that "delinking" from what he terms "the colonial matrix of power" (p. 9) is integral to confronting injustice and generating the conditions for a socially just praxis. The failings of the current normative order also offer opportunities to transform our teaching and learning practices and our relationships with one another. In the following section, I consider the ethical, relational, and methodological possibilities generated in this current moment of loss. In other words, if the normative neoliberal order is failing to meet the needs of children like Vinisha by sustaining unjust practices, how might we seek to generate distinctly different networks of support by foregrounding our interdependence with and amid diverse representations and embodiments of human experiences?

## TOWARD EQUITY AS PRAXIS AND CONFRONTING THE NECESSITY OF OUR INTERDEPENDENCIES

While I was reading all of the diagnoses, assessments, and evaluations describing Vinisha's ostensible failure to measure up, Vinisha joined our classroom. For the first couple of months our encounters could be characterized as discomforting and tenuous. Vinisha was extremely reluctant to connect with classmates and teachers. She shared little, if at all, about herself, her family, her interests, and her challenges, and she asked very few questions. These months did not offer a quick or easy solution to the tangible harm experienced when our education system remains committed to perpetuating the hegemony of the normative neoliberal subject. A classroom depends on the robust connections between children and teachers, and the latter are integral to establishing and sustaining a community that interacts with each other for several hours each day. A fundamental dilemma that must be confronted by early childhood educators is the way assessing children against normative developmental milestones limits the possibilities for fostering strong interdependent communities. Since Vinisha had already received the message from previous experiences with school that she was failing to measure up, how might her classmates and teachers find ways to refuse the detrimental impacts of this story while also inviting her to engage in the teaching and learning process?

There is a great deal of vibrant work being done in the field of ECE on different ways of interrupting, resisting, and transforming the hold childhood developmentalism continues to have in early years settings and classrooms across Canada (Berman & Abawi, 2019; Pacini-Ketchabaw & Pence, 2005). Referred to as **reconceptualist scholarship**, and drawing on various post-foundational theories—for example, post-structural and post-colonial concepts—one of the aims of such work is aptly described by Farley (2018) as a "critical examination of normative frames of development as they cut up and shape notions of childhood, but also, as they cut out particular narratives from the reality they construct" (p. 10). This kind of work has the potential to transform the teaching and learning relationships within which Vinisha and students like her are embedded. The work of reconceptualist scholarship points to the ways the current school structure is rooted in practices that are ready to cut out and erase Vinisha's contribution before she even enters the classroom. If we are to transform the conditions for teaching and learning, reconceptualist scholarship offers possibilities for refusing the exclusionary practices of the normative neoliberal order, while also stressing the need to attend to the complex ethical dilemmas that arise within our interdependent networks of teaching and learning.

The work of these ECE scholars demonstrates the strengths and limits of their approaches as it relates to children who are perpetually on the cusp of conditional inclusion or outright exclusion. One strength is the confrontation of the inevitable challenges of foregrounding our interdependencies within teaching and learning contexts. In part, these challenges are rooted in understanding the lived trauma that continues to be experienced while the normative neoliberal paradigm perpetuates its own dominance. For example, the work of Berry et al. (2018) and Pacini-Ketchabaw (2012) addresses the need to foreground our ethical relations while shifting our teaching and learning practices so as to inhabit complexly reconfigured interdependencies. According to Berry et al. (2018), one of the aims of this work involves "thinking-with others, with/in encounters [in order] to consider our positionalities with/in complex, messy interconnected ecologies" (p. 56). The significance of the insights offered here by Berry et al. (2018) and Pacini-Ketchabaw (2012) is that they emphasize the need for educators to attend to power imbalances within teaching and learning relationships. Attending to these power imbalances would prove to be integral to ensuring all children's contributions to our learning community were valued and valuable.

After the countless negative interactions Vinisha had in her first years of schooling, it should not surprise anyone that she was reluctant to engage, share, and connect with classmates or participate in activities. She needed time to trust that she was in a safe space and that her contribution in whatever form she chose to share it (e.g., oral, written, visual, a combination of the three) would be valued by her peers and teachers. Another significant strength of reconceptualist scholarship can be found in the attention given to the role of racism in the disproportional assessments of Black children as failures. For example, Ohito and Khoja-Moolji (2018) offer reparative readings of Black girls as a way to counter the "politics of respectability [that] rely on whiteness as the measuring stick for digestible forms of black woman-ness" (p. 280). Their analysis points to the persistent discrimination faced by Vinisha from her first experiences in kindergarten of being read as failing to measure up. It also points to the need for educators to confront and address the impacts of Vinisha's encounters with racism.

It took a couple of months before Vinisha was ready to share, contribute, and participate. In the meantime, we read stories together that featured characters encountering racism, classism, and sexism. Her classmates shared their own connections and experiences. And she slowly started to share pieces of herself. We learned about how much she loved spending time with her grandma when she visited Jamaica. We learned about her dad and how much she enjoyed spending time with him. She started to laugh and smile. She also started to talk about some of the negative experiences she had in her previous school. She loved to draw, and her drawings were often a starting point for connecting and sharing her ideas with others. She started to play with some of her classmates at recess. All of this took time as well as an understanding of the importance of fostering intersubjective teaching and learning encounters. Reconceptualist scholars Nxumalo and Cedillo (2017) consider the importance of enacting a "decolonial ethics" that would engage in a "questioning of what or whose knowledge counts in the making of a place and which past and present inhabitants of place count" (p. 104). At the time I was teaching and learning with Vinisha, I had neither heard of nor considered the importance of "decolonial ethics." However, that year we worked toward reassuring Vinisha that her knowledge and experiences were integral to the work of community building and place making.

Undoubtedly, there are many strengths and useful theoretical, ethical, methodological, and practical approaches within a reconceptualist framework. Specifically, this work may support ECE educators as they work to support Vinisha and her classmates to acknowledge and confront the ways we remain embedded in unjust colonial relations of power that disproportionally ensure that Vinisha will encounter schooling practices as always and already exclusionary and marginalizing. This was evident in Vinisha's exclusion from one school and her placement in another. Similarly, this is evident in a variety of methods of participation that include the option to refuse to participate by enacting silence, as Vinisha did for several months. Her silence in our classroom was encountered as a potent reminder for me of the need to question, refuse, and resist the normative neoliberal demand to perform the role of the productive student (e.g., by raising her hand or sharing answers to questions in order to demonstrate her understanding of the curriculum). Through her long period of silence, Vinisha enacted a refusal of voice and specifically of the demand to speak that is readily taken for granted within the normative demands of schooling. This offers every educator an opportunity to question and transform their teaching practice in order to make a substantive difference in the lives of young children like Vinisha, who encounter schooling as a place of conditional inclusion. The substantive difference is in the refusal and failure to perform the role of the neoliberal normative subject. It is the refusal to demand speech or voice and the ways in which such demands reinforce a conception of the self that repeatedly centres the logics of childhood developmentalism. Through its intent to decentre the neoliberal normative subject and confront structural racisms, the work of reconceptualist scholars and activists in ECE offers opportunities to provoke substantive change.

However, the work in this burgeoning and vibrant field needs to address a glaring limitation in its approaches. As several other disability studies scholars have shown, it is important to question and disrupt the taken-for-granted assumption that disability is indicative of lack and deficiency, an assumption that is ubiquitous in childhood developmental discourses and assessment practices. Disability and the ways in which it is integral to the human experience necessarily questions the normative order and the hegemony of the neoliberal subject. Excluding disability and disabled children like Vinisha from efforts to transform teaching and learning practices by enacting equity as praxis risks sustaining ableist logic, which remains one of the core tenets of the normative neoliberal order. Thus, I join Erevelles (2018), who effectively argues "that notwithstanding one's location on the axes of social difference, the ontology of disability … becomes the central analytic in articulating one's vision for social justice" (p. 68). Erevelles (2018) emphasizes the necessity of accepting disability as integral to our understanding of what it means to be human in our relationships with each other. In other words, disability and countless children who identify as disabled are not problems to be solved, managed, rehabilitated, or cured. Through the necessary "failure to become normate" (Mitchell et al., 2014, p. 300), disability and disabled children are integral to the teaching and learning process. Our relationship to disability, whether it be our own and/or that of a loved one, friend, colleague, or student, invites a questioning and refusal of the normative neoliberal order, and in so doing we can re-imagine what we mean to each other.

A component part of shifting and transforming the ontology of disability as integral to a socially just praxis is foregrounding the numerous contributions children with disabilities make within an interdependent teaching and learning context. As I mentioned earlier, it took a few months before Vinisha's justifiable reluctance to engage in teaching and learning with her classmates slowly shifted. Integral to this shift was supporting her use of visual aids, as well as encouraging Vinisha as she tried to communicate her ideas through mediums she felt most comfortable using. Inhabiting the silent refusal to become the neoliberal normative subject subsequently invites other non-hegemonic mediums of communication to flourish. Disability studies scholars like Erevelles (2018) and Mitchell et al. (2014) convey the significance of engaging with disability as vital to the project of refusal. In this way, disability studies scholarship and activism can form fruitful and productive connections with ECE scholars and practitioners in order "to draw out a complexly nuanced human constellation of meanings for crip/queer lives akin to other marginalized histories" (Mitchell et al., 2014, pp. 305–306). In other words, it is not only possible to forge a distinctly different set of interdependencies; it is also necessary if we are to generate the conditions for a fundamental transformation of our teaching and learning practices. The productive failure of students like Vinisha demonstrate not only the need for such a transformation, but also the potential benefits of forging new alliances between ECE and other critical fields of study.

## CONCLUDING THOUGHTS

Through an analysis of the detrimental impacts of ECE assessment practices embedded in discourses of childhood development, the purpose of this chapter has been to question, disrupt, resist, and refuse the hegemony of the normative neoliberal subject. Through the practice of current assessment protocols, children like Vinisha are consistently read as failing to measure up in a manner that sustains cycles of injustice, marginalization, and exclusion. A component part of confronting and refusing to engage in the endless repetition of this cycle has been to apply concepts from Haraway (2016), Tuck (2009), and Mignolo (2011). Similarly, I have considered the possibilities of highlighting interdependencies in ways that might transform teaching and learning relationships. Through the interventions of reconceptualist scholars within ECE, as well as the work of disability studies scholars, I have demonstrated the challenges, strengths, and limitations of foregrounding interdependent learning communities for student like Vinisha. One of the key contributions in this analysis has been to begin reading failure differently. Rather than as a lack or deficiency, I have considered here ways to read failure as urgently necessary and, ultimately, as a medium through which early childhood educators might produce new possibilities for learning in distinctly different ways. Integral to this invitation to explore new and more socially just ways of learning has been the infusion of disability, and specifically the experiences of disabled children, into the move away from the neoliberal subject and toward interconnected networks of teaching and learning. Paradoxically, it seems that cultivating the failure of the normative neoliberal subject generates the very conditions in which our learning communities can become available, accessible, and inclusive while also facing the complex challenges of our necessary connections.

## CRITICAL THINKING QUESTIONS

1. What is the relationship between the discourses and practices of child development and sustaining the hegemony of the normative neoliberal subject?
2. How do practices of observation and diagnosis sustain and generate the conditions for marginalization and exclusion?
3. How might educators embrace the failure of the normative neoliberal subject as an opportunity to transform teaching and learning relationships in a manner that foregrounds equity and social justice?

## GLOSSARY OF KEY TERMS

**disability studies:** A field of academic inquiry that opposes the study of disability through normative assumptions that discount and dehumanize children, youth, and adults that identify as disabled. Rather, disability studies questions the assumptions and norms of ableism and contends that disability is integral to human experiences and relationships

**normative neoliberal subject:** The Western, heteronormative, white, male, able-bodied, middle-class subject; the standard measure against which gradations of the human come to be counted as human.

**reconceptualist scholarship:** Scholarship focused on the importance of questioning normative assumptions by pointing out the exclusions and injustices generated in the hegemony of the normative neoliberal subject.

## REFERENCES

Abawi, Z., & Berman, R. (2019). Politicizing early childhood education and care in Ontario: Race, identity and belonging. *Journal of Curriculum, Teaching, Learning and Leadership in Education, 4*(2), 4–13.

Baker, B. (2015). From "somatic scandals" to "a constant potential for violence"? The culture of dissection, brain-based learning, and the rewriting/rewiring of "the child." *Journal of Curriculum and Pedagogy, 12*(2), 168–197.

Berman, R., & Abawi, Z. (2019). Thinking and doing otherwise: Reconceptualist contributions to early childhood education and care. In S. Jagger (Ed.), *History and philosophy of early years education and care: Canadian perspectives* (pp. 165–199). Canadian Scholars.

Berry, A., Do Nascimento, A., & Pacini-Ketchabaw, V. (2018). Pedagogies of care: Thinking-with and paying attention. *International Child and Youth Care Network, 235*, 49–57.

Ellis, J. (2019). *A class by themselves? The origins of special education in Toronto and beyond*. University of Toronto Press.

Erevelles, N. (2000). Educating unruly bodies: Critical pedagogy, disability studies, and the politics of schooling. *Educational Theory, 50*(1), 25–47.

Erevelles, N. (2005). Understanding curriculum as normalizing text: Disability studies meet curriculum theory. *Journal of Curriculum Studies, 37*(4), 421–439.

Erevelles, N. (2018). Toward justice as ontology: Disability and the question of (in)difference. In E. Tuck & W. Yang (Eds.), *Toward what justice?* (pp. 67–83). Routledge.

Farley, L. (2018). *Childhood beyond pathology: A psychoanalytic study of development and diagnosis*. SUNY Press.

Halberstam, J. (2011). *The queer art of failure*. Duke University Press.

Haraway, D. J. (2016). *Staying with the trouble: Making kin in the Chthulucene*. Duke University Press.

MacLure, M., Holmes, R., Jones, L., & MacRae, C. (2010). Silence as resistance to analysis: Or on not opening one's mouth properly. *Qualitative Inquiry, 16*(6), 492–500.

MacNevin, M., & Berman, R. (2017). The Black baby doll doesn't fit the disconnect between early childhood diversity policy, early childhood educator practice, and children's play. *Early Child Development and Care, 187*(5–6), 827–839.

McGuire, A. (2017). De-regulating disorder: On the rise of the spectrum as a neoliberal metric of human value. *Journal of Literary & Cultural Disability Studies, 11*(4), 403–421.

Michalko, R. (2002). *The difference that disability makes.* Temple University Press.

Mignolo, W. (2011). *The darker side of Western modernity: Global futures, decolonial options.* Duke University Press.

Mitchell, D. T., Snyder, S. L., & Ware, L. (2014). "[Every] child left behind": Curricular cripistemologies and the crip/queer art of failure. *Journal of Literary & Cultural Disability Studies, 8*(3), 295–314.

Nxumalo, F., & Cedillo, S. (2017). Decolonizing place in early childhood studies: Thinking with Indigenous onto-epistemologies and Black feminist geographies. *Global Studies of Childhood, 7*(2), 99–112.

Ohito, E. O., & Khoja-Moolji, S. (2018). Reparative readings: Re-claiming Black feminised bodies as sites of somatic pleasures and possibilities. *Gender and Education, 30*(3), 277–294.

Pacini-Ketchabaw, V. (2012). Postcolonial entanglements: Unruling stories. *Child & Youth Services, 33*(3–4), 303–316.

Pacini-Ketchabaw, V., & Pence, A. (2005). Contextualizing the reconceptualist movement in Canadian early childhood education. In V. Pacini-Ketchabaw & A. Pence (Eds.), *Research connections Canada: Vol. 13. Supporting children and families* (pp. 5–20). Canadian Child Care Federation.

Portelli, J. P., & Eizadirad, A. (2018). Subversion in education: Common misunderstandings & myths. *International Journal of Critical Pedagogy, 9*(1), 54–72.

Slee, R. (2019). Belonging in an age of exclusion. *International Journal of Inclusive Education, 23*(9), 909–922.

Stephens, E., & Cryle, P. (2017). Eugenics and the normal body: The role of visual images and intelligence testing in framing the treatment of people with disabilities in the early twentieth century. *Continuum, 31*(3), 365–376.

Tuck, E. (2009). Suspending damage: A letter to communities. *Harvard Educational Review, 79*(3), 409–428.

Walkerdine, V. (1993). Beyond developmentalism? *Theory & Psychology, 3*(4), 451–469.

CHAPTER 9

# Reflect, Enact, and Transform: A Preliminary Anti-Racism Guide for Early Childhood Educators

*Kerry–Ann Escayg*

## LEARNING OBJECTIVES

- To discuss and contextualize anti-racist teaching practices within an analysis of anti-Black racism in Canada
- To develop critical self-reflection skills pertinent to both professional and self-development
- To recognize the intersections between teacher identity and professional practices

## INTRODUCTION

What are the qualities of an effective educator? Patience? Respect? Creativity? Kindness? Compassion? These are all important, but let's take it a step further. **Racism** is systematic and pervasive throughout Canada. How should you respond? Can you either explain or define racism? As an educator, do you care about racial justice? This chapter reviews racism in Canada, with a particular focus on **anti-Black racism**. The goal is to encourage you, the reader, to consider how the school system is deeply entrenched in a historical legacy of anti-Black racism, and to identify and critique the intersections of identity, discourse, and teaching practice. Anti-racist pedagogy stems from an anti-racist identity, so challenging racial inequities at all levels of education requires that educators—especially white educators—question their understandings of race and racism and then develop sound anti-racist practices. This is especially important in early childhood education, as young children begin to acquire an astute awareness of race and racial privilege.

Early socialization in a predominantly white environment contributes to the development of the "White racial frame" (Feagin, 2010), which informs teaching practices and decisions that impede educational success and social-emotional well-being among children of colour (Escayg, 2020). Drawing from ecological theory, scholars in the United States have explored the psychological consequences of racism in schools, including racial trauma among Black children and adolescents (Jernigan, 2009; Jernigan & Daniel, 2011; Saleem et al., 2020). Few scholars have explored racial trauma among racialized children in Canada, especially in educational contexts, but research suggests that Canadian children likely encounter similar unwelcoming classroom spaces (e.g., Daniel & Escayg, 2019; James & Turner, 2017).

This chapter begins with a discussion of racism in Canada, with a particular focus on anti-Black racism. It explores the convergences between the theoretical and empirical literature on racism and offers action steps/reflective prompts that can stimulate deep reflection about teaching and learning in relation to racism in Canada and anti-racist pedagogy. It concludes with a brief overview of the qualities of an anti-racist early childhood educator.

## PRESENT BUT DENIED: HISTORICAL AND CONTEMPORARY RACISM IN ONTARIO AND CANADA

In contrast to prevailing societal views, the scholarly literature clearly reveals a long-standing history of racism in Canada. As Nelson and Nelson (2004) commented, "The racism that many people of colour and

First Nations often face, whether institutional or informal, is often met with the denial of white Canadians, who insist that these experiences are not representative of their Canada" (p. 2). For the purposes of this chapter, *racism* refers to a collective of institutional and individual practices that use socially constructed meanings of race to create and sustain privilege and power for the dominant group (white Canadians). In short, racism is power.

Canadians tend to maintain naive beliefs about racial equality, despite the country's history of coerced acquisition of Indigenous lands and the subsequent forced labour of First Nations people, along with the establishment of residential schools (Dei, 2005). Another example of racism in Canada's social and legal history is the treatment of African-Canadians, including discriminatory laws that precluded their access to essential services, such as education. The enforcement of legal authority to marginalize and discriminate on the grounds of race was a common feature in the experiences of new Canadians in the nineteenth century (Blackhouse, 1999).

The history of slavery in Canada is not widely known. The silencing of this national sin is arguably a type of collective amnesia, typified by an inclination to dismiss and ignore the cumulative impact of institutionalized and racialized subjugation. Indeed, Cooper (2007) has referred to slavery as "Canada's best kept secret" (p. 68). However, historical records bear witness to the existence of slavery in Canada—and the experiences of the enslaved.

Slavery in Canada commenced in 1628 and ended in 1833 (Cooper, 2007). This history is complex. In 1688, Jean Bochart de Champigny requested permission from Louis XIV to introduce Black slaves into the colony of New France (Cooper, 2007). Slavery was legal in what is now Canada from 1689 to 1709 (Winks, 1997), even though the practice continued for much longer. Both French and British colonists supported and practised slavery (Cooper, 2007). Slavery in Canada differed somewhat from that in the United States; for example, "slaves in Canada engaged in a variety of occupations from rat catcher to hangman—but most worked as house servants, as farm labourers, or in skilled occupations" (Elgersman, 2013, p. 77).

Members of elite bourgeois society in New France and British Canada purchased slaves; this was especially true of members of the church, nobility, merchants, lawyers, government officials, and gentry (Copper, 2007, p. 77). Most slaveholders were French, and they came especially from the merchant elite (Cooper, 2007; Winks, 1997).

Enslaved individuals were subjected to daily assault on the mind, body, and spirit, which led to a variety of subversive acts. As Cooper (2007) writes, "they ran away, talked back, broke tools, were disobedient, threated their owners, organized slave uprisings, and in two cases, allegedly set major fires that devastated colonial towns" (p. 81). Whether it was due to exasperated energies, a burdened soul, or a psyche that refused to acquiesce to the expectations of deference to white control, a culture of resistance emerged from this continued dehumanization. This lived practice of resistance was antithetical to the goals of a racialized system of control and the ideology on which it was built. Enslaved people in Canada, similar to their counterparts in the United States and the Caribbean, actively challenged and resisted the yoke of slavery. Slavery was abolished in all British colonies in 1833, but the passage of time has done little to diminish the wide-scale anti-Black discourse that continues to rationalize discriminatory practices. Although less overt, anti-Black racism still pervades Canadian institutions and society.

## ANTI-BLACK RACISM

Anti-Black racism is one component of the broader construct of racism, which is related to the forces of power relations and white privilege. Anti-Black racism refers to actions, beliefs, and institutional practices that limit the life chances and opportunities of Blacks. One of the chief characteristics of anti-Black racism is violence—both physical (i.e., police brutality, death, and overt racist attacks) and psychological (i.e., racial discourse related to the inferiority of Black identity).

From an ideological standpoint, anti-Black racism emerges from socially constructed meanings of Blackness that link the Black body with criminality, deviance, and other race-based pathologies (Feagin,

2013; Mullings et al., 2016). It began with slavery, but contemporary systemic racism and anti-Black rhetoric continues to position Blackness as an "other." The result is an unfounded "fear of the Black body" (Mullings et al., 2016, p. 25), which, in the court of public opinion, is thought to be bereft of humanity and, therefore, worthy of punishment and violence.

Blacks, especially African-American and African-Canadian males, are largely portrayed as objects rather than persons, as criminals rather than citizens. The ideologies and images commonly disseminated in the media support excessive policing, surveillance, punishment, and incarceration rates that far exceed those of the broader population (Alexander, 2012; Mullings et al., 2016; Tanovich, 2006; Welch, 2007). Such effects, however, extend beyond the scope of the criminal-justice system. Anti-Black racism directly affects the social existence and psychological well-being of Blacks, including Black Canadians.

Some Canadian research has revealed the multiple ways in which anti-Black racism manifests in the classroom, and the effect this has on the quality of educational experiences for Black children and youth. For example, dominant racial stereotypes are known to influence how teachers perceive Black students: they have lower academic expectations for their Black students, which contributes to the overrepresentation of Black students in remedial as opposed to gifted classes (James, 2019; James & Turner, 2017). Black students are also suspended and expelled, or less formally pushed out of school, more frequently than their white peers (Dei, 2008).

In addition to biased disciplinary practices, a Eurocentric curriculum is known to affect the engagement of Black students, as well as their attitude to learning, and ultimately their academic success. Dei and James (2002) concluded that institutionalized exclusion operates through curricula that fail to centre the racial and cultural identities of students. In a more optimistic vein, Henry (2017) writes that "curriculum can be powerful. It can be a way of undoing the deleterious effects of living in a society where one is excluded and made to feel that he/she has not made any important contributions" (p. 10). Thus, while curriculum can and does serve to perpetuate anti-Black racism in the classroom, and often reproduces deeply rooted systemic inequities, it can also be reframed as a pedagogical device for healing and promoting positive racial identity and self-esteem among Black/African-Canadian students.

## NOW WHAT? A PRELIMINARY SELF-REFLECTIVE GUIDE FOR ANTI-RACIST PROFESSIONAL PRACTICE

Anti-racism is a lifelong journey requiring sustained commitment and a tenacity to endure despite persecution (both professional and personal). It is rewarding, but it also involves risks. Those who seek to redress normative ways of schooling, social relations, and the systems underpinning white privilege face resistance—hostile resistance. Those engaging in anti-racism practices—at the educational, scholarly, or community grassroots level—must be brave. They may be motivated by a love of justice or humanity; regardless, anti-racist efforts and global systemic change require moral integrity and hard work. The battle has been waged for a long time, and we as educators and scholars need to continue the fight—beginning with self-reflection.

This brings us back to our earlier question: What are the qualities of an effective educator? After reading the brief discussion of racism in Canada presented above, how might you change specific areas of your teaching? The next section presents some ways to engage in self-reflection within the context of systemic racism and anti-Black stereotypes, which can have direct implications for anti-racist teaching practices.

## SYSTEMIC INEQUITIES AND IMPLICATIONS FOR TEACHING

Blacks and other racialized populations in Canada face systemic racism; these discriminatory practices and policies result in financial, professional, and educational disparities. One example is the income inequality between racialized and white Canadians. Drawing from census data, the authors of one recent study reported that "the overall earnings gap between racialized and non-racialized men and racialized and non-racialized women has remained virtually unchanged since 2006" (Block et al., 2019, p. 13). Such disparities may be attributed to racist practices within the labour market; many studies have shown that Black Canadians encounter significant discrimination in the job market and the workplace (Branker, 2017; Briggs, 2018; Henry & Ginzberg, 1985). The disproportionate poverty levels, and in particular, child poverty levels experienced by racialized, Indigenous, and Black children in Toronto, Ontario (e.g., Polanyi et al., 2017), further illustrate the interconnected systems that characterize racism—as well as the "colour" of economic injustice.

Families and children are affected in many ways by impoverished socio-economic conditions. Poverty hinders the ability of parents to secure safe and affordable housing and provide adequate nutrition and other daily needs. Neighbourhood environments, especially unsafe environments, also affect the health and well-being of children (Jensen, 2009). Many studies have shown that poverty affects children's cognitive development, language development, and social-emotional functioning (Brooks-Gunn & Duncan, 1997; Noble et al., 2015; Pungello et al., 2009). In highlighting the realities faced by impoverished families and children, the goal here is not to endorse a deficit perspective, but rather to expose the unjust nature of class and racial inequalities and underscore the importance of teaching from an anti-racist perspective that gives credence to the experiences embodied in dual and often multiple positionalities, including race, gender, and class.

The self-reflective prompts provided in box 9.1 are derived from my own elementary and early childhood teaching experiences in schools characterized by their low socio-economic status, as well as the scholarly literature. They are designed to help you consider how you could approach teaching from a perspective that recognizes the lived realities of children and families, including the structural barriers and stressors they experience on a daily basis. The goal is for you to interrogate your own perceptions about the poor, to humanize the marginalized, and

## Box 9.1

Professional Practice Prompts:

1. It is parent-teacher night. One student in your class is performing below their grade level. You invited the parent to attend the parent-teacher night, but you have not yet received a response. You have tried several times to meet with the parent but have not been successful. How do you view this parent? What are the reasons for your perception?

2. A kindergarten student is exhibiting poor social-emotional skills. Specifically, they act out, are impulsive, and fail to follow class-room instructions. What do you believe are the reasons for these behaviours?

Self-Reflection Prompt:

1. Budge and Parrett (2018) write that "poverty is primarily caused by conditions in the broader society (including schools) that create unequal opportunities" (p. 7). Do you agree or disagree? Provide a detailed rationale for your response.

to be more compassionate toward racialized children and the familial contexts in which they are raised.

## ANTI-RACIST PEDAGOGY AS TRANSFORMATION: CURRICULUM AS COUNTER-NARRATIVE

Racial stereotypes, particularly those regarding Black males, are common throughout Canada and the United States. Some scholars have linked these to the overrepresentation of Black males in prisons, as well as to the higher suspension and expulsion rates among Black males and females. Less research has focused on the intersections of race, disciplinary practices, and educational outcomes in Canada compared to the United States, but the available research reveals significant parallels. Based on data from the Toronto District School Board and consultations with youth, parents, community, educators, and administrators, James and Turner (2017) found that anti-Black racism permeated many areas of teachers' professional practice. For example, Black students were subjected to harsher disciplinary measures than their white peers. One research participant said, "At age seven, I was playing fight with a boy and punched him. The teacher told me you can go to jail for that" (James & Turner, 2017, p. 56), illustrating how the teacher superimposed underlying racial biases on a typical play episode between two children. In this way, racism functions to deny Black children their childhood; they are viewed as adults, not children. This makes it vital for educators to self-reflect on how they may have internalized racist images and stereotypes—the "White racial frame" (Escayg, 2020; Feagin, 2010)—to avoid differential treatment of Black children and youth in classrooms and the broader school system.

The disciplining of the Black body and mind encompasses more than the restrictive and punitive measures discussed above. Eurocentric curriculum and classroom environments further contribute to Black students' experience of isolation in school contexts (James & Turner, 2017). In contrast, African-centred curricula can attenuate educational inequities and the psychological effects of systemic racism by developing racial pride among Black students, which, in turn, can foster their academic success (Dei & Kempf, 2013; Howard & James, 2019). In an early childhood context, for example, an African-centred curriculum can encourage Black children to express themselves in ways congruent with their cultural ways of being and knowing. A school curriculum can and should be transformative.

## Box 9.2

Professional Practice Prompts:

1. Analyze your disciplinary practices. First, start a running record of how often you discipline Black children (male and female). What were the antecedents of the child's behaviour? How did you respond to the child's behaviour?

2. For early childhood educators in play-based classrooms: Consider the statement of the participant in the study by James and Turner (2017). Is there a racial factor underlying how you interpret the play of Black boys?

3. Examine your classroom environment and curriculum (images, books, posters, etc.). Is it a "race-silenced" space? If so, what is the reason for failure to create an anti-racist learning space? Do you discuss race/racism with children? Provide a rationale for your response.

Self-Reflection Prompts:

1. What is the function of racial stereotypes, particularly stereotypes about Black males in the Canadian context?

2. How do racial stereotypes undergird systemic racism?

3. How have you challenged (professionally or personally) stereotypes about Black males?

4. Are you familiar with counter-narratives that contradict dominant racial stereotypes?

## WHAT DOES IT MEAN TO BE AN ANTI-RACIST EDUCATOR?

Anti-racist educators advance racial justice through social, political, and educational activism. They have a comprehensive understanding of racism, including how it has evolved over the years, and use this information to guide their teaching practice as well as their interactions in everyday life. Specifically, they challenge colour-blindness by recognizing and giving validity to the lived experiences and cultural and racial identities of racialized students. They encourage white students to confront and critique racial privilege and oppression. In anti-racist classrooms, white educators are acutely conscious of their own identity and how it can affect pedagogy, curriculum decisions, and parent-teacher partnerships.

Anti-racist educators do not perceive the classroom or the school as an apolitical or neutral space. Rather, they work toward anti-racist transformation and, by extension, equitable learning opportunities for students. They consider how the classroom environment can cultivate social-political consciousness in all students, and they openly and willingly infuse learning activities with discussions of race and racism. In short, anti-racist educators are agents of change—within the classroom and in the broader society.

Self-reflection is a significant component of becoming an anti-racist educator. This is particularly the case for white educators, who must consistently seek professional learning opportunities to help unpack white socialization experiences, privilege (and the many dimensions of privilege, including psychological, material, and cultural elements), and power. They should learn from others, work to abolish their own "White fragility" (DiAngelo, 2018), and not silence or dismiss marginalized voices.

Specific techniques used by anti-racist white educators include reflecting on the extent to which they have internalized the myth of white superiority, and in the process interrogating the meanings they have assigned—either consciously or unconsciously—to their white identity. They also actively employ humility during cross-racial interactions and anti-racist collaborations with racialized educators/scholars. They avoid framing discussions from a perspective that eclipses the voice of racialized groups while centring white "reactive" responses, because this is a form of epistemic violence manifesting white privilege. In contrast, they should use their privilege to advocate for racialized students and families, confront racist jokes/comments by peers, and work with administration/leadership to provide ongoing anti-racist professional training opportunities. Anti-racist educators remain steadfast in the face of systemic racism; they are revolutionaries with a passion for justice.

In conclusion, this chapter has provided a short guide for anti-racist educators along with an overview of research about historical systemic and anti-Black racism in Canada. This discussion is both necessary and timely. Recent global events have demonstrated that resistance to racial injustice cannot be deferred until later. We should not have to ask another generation of impassioned justice-seekers to step onto the battlefield of honour to reassert their rights to equity, dignity, and respect. Many such visionaries have already fought for the well-being of others, both in Canada and globally, motivated by a desire for justice. What is your role? How will you self-reflect? Will you employ anti-racist practices in your classroom? One thing is certain: silence is definitely not the answer.

## CRITICAL THINKING QUESTIONS

1. How do dominant discourses and stereotypes of Black Canadians subsequently deprive Black children of their childhood, particularly in educational spaces?
2. How might pedagogy be a site of resistance aimed at healing and promoting a positive racial identity among Black students?

## GLOSSARY OF KEY TERMS

**anti-Black racism:** Buttressed by racial stereotypes, anti-Black racism encompasses historical and contemporary ideologies, beliefs, and institutionalized practices integral to various forms of racial oppression, as well as systemic, physical, and psychological violence against the Black body.

**racism:** An interconnected system of individual, institutional, and cultural practices that obtain economic, social, and psychological advantages for the dominant group. Underpinning such a system is the meaning attached to race.

# REFERENCES

Alexander, M. (2012). *The new Jim Crow: Mass incarceration in the age of colorblindness.* The New Press.

Blackhouse, C. (1999). *Colour-coded: A legal history of racism in Canada, 1990–1950.* University of Toronto Press.

Block, S., Galabuzi, G., & Tranjan, R. (2019). *Canada's colour coded income inequality.* Canadian Centre for Policy Alternatives.

Branker, R. R. (2017). Labour market discrimination: The lived experiences of English-speaking Caribbean immigrants in Toronto. *Journal of International Migration and Integration, 18*(1), 203–222.

Briggs, A. Q. (2018). Second generation Caribbean Black male youths discuss obstacles to educational and employment opportunities: A critical race counter-narrative analysis. *Journal of Youth Studies, 21*(4), 533–549.

Brooks-Gunn, J., & Duncan, G. J. (1997). The effects of poverty on children. *The Future of Children, 7*(2), 55–71.

Budge, K., & Parrett, W. (2018). *Disrupting poverty: Five powerful classroom practices.* Association for Supervision and Curriculum Development.

Cooper, A. (2007). *The hanging of Angelique: The untold story of Canadian slavery and the burning of Old Montreal.* University of Georgia Press.

Daniel, B. J. J., & Escayg, K.-A. (2019). "But, I don't believe it's about race": Challenging fallacies of race and racism amongst early childhood educators in Ontario. *Journal of Curriculum, Teaching, Learning and Leadership in Education, 4*(2), 14–28.

Dei, G. J. S. (2005). Racism in Canadian contexts: Exploring public and private issues in the educational system. In W. J. Tettey & K. P. Puplampu (Eds.), *The African diaspora in Canada: Negotiating identity and belonging* (pp. 93–112). University of Calgary Press.

Dei, G. J. S. (2008). Schooling as community: Race, schooling, and the education of African youth. *Journal of Black Studies, 38*(3), 346–366.

Dei, G. J. S., & James, I. M. (2002). Beyond the rhetoric: Moving from exclusion, reaching for inclusion in Canadian schools. *Alberta Journal of Educational Research, 48*(1), 61–87.

Dei, G. J. S., & Kempf, A. (2013). *New perspectives on African-centred education in Canada.* Canadian Scholars' Press.

DiAngelo, R. (2018). *White fragility: Why it's so hard for white people to talk about racism*. Beacon Press.

Elgersman, M. G. (2013). *Unyielding spirits: Black women and slavery in early Canada and Jamaica*. Routledge.

Escayg, K.-A. (2020). Anti-racism in U.S. early childhood education: Foundational principles. *Sociology Compass, 14*(4), 1–15.

Feagin, J. R. (2010). *The white racial frame: Centuries of framing and counter-framing*. Routledge.

Feagin, J. R. (2013). *Systemic racism: A theory of oppression*. Routledge.

Henry, A. (2017). Culturally relevant pedagogy in Canada: Reflections regarding Black students. *Teachers College Record, 119*(1). http://www.tcrecord.org/library/abstract.asp?contentid=21716

Henry, F., & Ginzberg, E. (1985). *Who gets the work? A test of racial discrimination in employment*. Urban Alliance on Race Relations and the Social Planning Council of Metropolitan Toronto.

Howard, P. S., & James, C. E. (2019). When dreams take flight: How teachers imagine and implement an environment that nurtures Blackness at an Africentric school in Toronto, Ontario. *Curriculum Inquiry, 49*(3), 313–337.

James, C. (2019). Adapting, disrupting, and resisting: How middle school Black males position themselves in response to racialization in school. *Canadian Journal of Sociology, 44*(4), 373–398.

James, C. E., & Turner, T. (2017). *Towards race equity in education: The schooling of Black students in the Greater Toronto Area*. York University.

Jensen, E. (2009). *Teaching with poverty in mind: What being poor does to kids' brains and what schools can do about it*. Association for Supervision and Curriculum Development.

Jernigan, M. M. (2009). Using a Sankofa intervention to influence Black girls' racial identity development and school-related experiences. *Dissertation Abstracts International Section A: Humanities and Social Sciences, 70*(2-A), 472. https://dlib.bc.edu/islandora/object/bc-ir:101827

Jernigan, M. M., & Daniel, J. H. (2011). Racial trauma in the lives of Black children and adolescents: Challenges and clinical implications. *Journal of Child & Adolescent Trauma, 4*(2), 123–141.

Mullings, D. V., Morgan, A., & Quelleng, H. K. (2016). Canada the great white north where anti-black racism thrives: Kicking down the doors and exposing the realities. *Phylon, 53*(1), 20–41.

Nelson, C., & Nelson, C. A. (Eds.). (2004). *Racism, eh? A critical inter-disciplinary anthology of race and racism in Canada.* Captus Press.

Noble, K. G., Houston, S. M., Brito, N. H., Bartsch, H., Kan, E., Kuperman, J. M., … & Schork, N. J. (2015). Family income, parental education and brain structure in children and adolescents. *Nature Neuroscience, 18*(5), 773–778.

Polanyi, M., Wilson, B., Mustachi, J., Ekra, M., & Kerr, M. (2017). *Unequal city: The hidden divide among Toronto's children and youth.* Children's Aid Society of Toronto. http://torontocas.ca/sites/torontocas/files/CAST%20Child%20Poverty%20Report%20Nov%202017.pdf

Pungello, E. P., Iruka, I. U., Dotterer, A. M., Mills-Koonce, R., & Reznick, J. S. (2009). The effects of socioeconomic status, race, and parenting on language development in early childhood. *Developmental Psychology, 45*(2), 544–557.

Saleem, F. T., Anderson, R. E., & Williams, M. (2020). Addressing the "myth" of racial trauma: Developmental and ecological considerations for youth of color. *Clinical Child and Family Psychology Review, 23*(1), 1–14.

Tanovich, D. (2006). *The colour of justice: Policing race in Canada.* Irwin Law.

Welch, K. (2007). Black criminal stereotypes and racial profiling. *Journal of Contemporary Criminal Justice, 23*(3), 276–288.

Winks, R. W. (1997). *Blacks in Canada: A history.* McGill-Queen's University Press.

CONCLUSION

# Some Concluding Thoughts on Equity as Praxis

*Rachel Berman*

At the outset of this book, the three editors invited you, the reader, to actively engage with the content by critically self-examining your own social location(s) of privilege and the oppression situated in your personal and ancestral histories. We encouraged you to think about your own ideas and notions of children and childhood, and to (un)learn, relearn, disrupt, resist, and subvert exclusively psychological-developmentalist norms that dominate depictions of childhood and early learning pedagogies and epistemologies via the alternative approaches and rethinking that was discussed throughout this text. This book is certainly not the first to urge the field of early childhood education and care (ECEC) to rethink the frameworks that dominate thinking and practice in this field, and we hope that we have added to and expanded the conversation about the need to reconceptualize the field of ECEC.

As you leave this book, although we hope you will return and revisit various chapters, we hope you have been challenged to rethink assumptions and to re-envision ways of being in relationship with children and families. We also hope some of you saw yourselves in the pages of this text as some of the voices and perspectives, ideas and frameworks that are often relegated to the margins of ECEC, if they are acknowledged at all, were taken up. We hope you agree, if you did not before, that we can no longer rely on acontextual, colonial, and colour-blind frameworks for working with children and families in ECEC. We can no longer be satisfied with being told that some ways of thinking are too complicated or too difficult or too unruly. We hope you are motivated to work with the knowledge in this book as we move into ever more challenging times. Given the inequities revealed by the COVID-19 pandemic, this work is more important than ever.

By considering and critiquing your understandings of children, families, and communities, and of practices in ECEC, this text has sought to provide alternative strength-based approaches for critical and transformative praxis. This can only be done via "reflection and action upon the world in order to transform it" (Freire, 1970, p. 51).

## REFERENCE

Freire, P. (1970). *Pedagogy of the oppressed*. Continuum.

# CONTRIBUTOR BIOGRAPHIES

**Zuhra Abawi** is an assistant professor in the College of Education at Niagara University in Ontario. Before joining Niagara as a full-time faculty member, she also taught at Ryerson University's School of Early Childhood Studies and Western University's Faculty of Education. She was also an elementary teacher and early childhood educator. She received her doctorate in education from the Ontario Institute for Studies in Education, University of Toronto. Her research interests include early childhood education and care, teacher education, and race and identity in education and educational policy. She is the author of the forthcoming *The Effectiveness of Educational Policy for Bias-Free Teacher Hiring: Critical Insights to Enhance Diversity in the Canadian Teacher Workforce* (Routledge Research in Educational Equality and Diversity, 2021).

**Rachel Berman** is a white settler who was born in the United States and grew up in Toronto, Ontario, the traditional territory of many nations, including the Mississaugas of the New Credit, the Anishinaabe, the Chippewa, the Haudenosaunee, and the Wendat peoples; it is covered by Treaty 13. Dr. Berman is an associate professor and the graduate program director in the School of Early Childhood Studies at Ryerson University and an adjunct member of the Graduate Program in Gender, Feminist and Women's Studies at York University. Her research and teaching focus on "race" in early childhood settings; family engagement; theoretical frameworks in early childhood studies, in particular critical race theory and feminist theories; and critical qualitative methods, including social research with children. Her research has appeared in the *International Critical Childhood Policy Studies Journal*, the *Journal of Childhood Studies*, *Children & Society*, and the *International Journal of Qualitative Methods*, among others.

**Ardavan Eizadirad** is an assistant professor in the Faculty of Education at Wilfrid Laurier University, and an instructor in the School of Early

Childhood Studies at Ryerson University and the Faculty of Social Work at the University of Toronto. He is an educator with the Toronto District School Board and author of *Decolonizing Educational Assessment: Ontario Elementary Students and the EQAO* (Palgrave Macmillan, 2019). His research interests include equity, standardized testing, systems of accountability, community engagement, anti-oppressive practices, critical pedagogy, social justice education, resistance, subversion, and decolonization. Dr. Eizadirad is also the founder of EDIcation Consulting (www.edication.org), which offers equity, diversity, and inclusion training to organizations.

---

**Judith K. Bernhard** is a full professor in Ryerson University's School of Early Childhood Studies with over 25 years of teaching and research experience. Her work focuses on the areas of diversity, inclusion, and the settlement of newcomer children and families in early childhood settings. Dr. Bernhard is affiliated with Ryerson's Master of Arts in Immigration and Settlement Studies.

**Alana Butler** is an assistant professor in the Faculty of Education at Queen's University in Kingston, Ontario. In 2015, she graduated with a PhD in education from Cornell University in Ithaca, New York. Her research interests include the academic achievement of students of low socio-economic status, race and schooling, equity and inclusion, and multicultural education. In 2019, she was awarded an Insight Development Grant from the Social Sciences and Humanities Research Council of Canada for her study entitled *Beating the Odds: An Intergenerational Examination of Cultural Barriers to Postsecondary Education for Low Income Ontario Youth*.

**Adam Davies** is an interdisciplinary critical scholar and an assistant professor in the Graduate Program in Family Relations and Human Development at the University of Guelph. He recently finished his PhD in curriculum studies and teacher development and sexual diversity studies at the Ontario Institute for Studies in Education, University of Toronto. Dr. Davies's work focuses upon early childhood education and care, queer and trans studies in schooling, the sociology of childhood and youth studies, critical disability studies, and gendered regulation within queer men's online communities.

**Kerry-Ann Escayg** is an assistant professor at the College of Education at the University of Nebraska Omaha. Her research focuses on anti-racism in early childhood education as well as children and race. As a social theorist, Dr. Escayg has utilized elements of critical race theory, Black feminist thought, and anti-racist education to offer new exegeses on children's racial identity development, including strategies to promote positive racial identity among Black children; a research-derived protocol to assess children's play; and an anti-racist approach to US early childhood education. Her recent publications have highlighted and interrogated the ways in which whiteness, as a system of racial privilege, functions in early childhood contexts. Central to Dr. Escayg's work is a commitment to racial equity in the early years and the holistic well-being of children of colour, and Black children in particular. In addition to her scholarly and activist pursuits, Dr. Escayg writes short stories, poetry, and children's literature.

**Rhea Ashley Hoskin** is an interdisciplinary feminist sociologist and an Ontario Women's Health Scholar working as a post-doctoral researcher in the Departments of Gender Studies and Psychology at Queen's University. Rhea's work focuses on femininities, femme theory, femme identities, critical femininities, and femmephobia. In particular, her work examines perceptions of femininity and sources of prejudice rooted in the devaluing or regulation of femininity.

**Lisa Johnston** is a registered early childhood educator, field liaison, and part-time instructor with the School of Early Childhood at George Brown College in Toronto. She holds an MA in early childhood studies from Ryerson University and is embarking on a PhD at York University. She has 17 years of experience in George Brown College's Lab

Schools working with children and families and mentoring early childhood education students. Lisa is a passionate educator-activist and citizen-scientist, an avid hiker, and a musician. She is deeply immersed in pedagogical thinking that reconceptualizes early childhood education and asks how we can live well with others.

**Maria Karmiris** received her PhD in 2019 from the Department of Social Justice Education at the University of Toronto. She has been teaching elementary school in the Toronto District School Board since 2002. Since 2019, she also has been teaching as a contract lecturer in Ryerson University's School of Early Childhood Studies and School of Disability Studies. Her work uses concepts, methods, and methodologies from critical disability studies, post-colonial studies, decolonial studies, and post-structural feminisms in order to delve into issues of inequity and injustice within education.

**Rachel Langford** is a professor emeritus in the School of Early Childhood Studies at Ryerson University. She is the principal investigator of an SSHRC-awarded project that seeks to theorize and frame a robust and coherent integration of care, ethics of care, and care work into Canadian child-care advocacy, policy, and practice. She is a co-editor of *Caring for Children: Social Movements and Public Policy in Canada* (UBC Press, 2017), and the editor of an anthology, *Theorizing Feminist Ethics of Care in Early Childhood Practice: Possibilities and Dangers* (Bloomsbury Academic Press, 2019).

**Nidhi Menon** started her journey learning about and with children in India and received her master's in early childhood education in the United States before working in various early childhood settings in Canada. Her research interests are informed by her personal experiences and understanding of migration and mobility, her social location, and her constant curiosity about children and their impact on our world. She is currently doing a PhD at the Ontario Institute for Studies in Education, University of Toronto. Her scholarship is situated at the intersections of post-structural and Third World feminisms, the new sociology of childhood, unequal childhoods, and issues of power in early childhood experiences.

**Alana Powell** is policy and special projects officer at the Association of Early Childhood Educators Ontario. Alana completed her MA in early childhood studies at Ryerson University and is a registered early childhood educator. Prior to her role at the Association of Early Childhood Educators Ontario, she was a contract lecturer in George Brown College's School of Early Childhood. Her research engages in critical exploration of care discourses in early childhood, and she has played an active role in the Ontario child-care advocacy movement for several years.

**Maya-Rose Simon** is a tribal-enrolled Native American from the Chippewa Tribe of Sault Ste. Marie. Simon has a bachelor of child development (honours) and an ECE diploma. She has more than 20 years' experience as an educator teaching infant to school-age children. She is also a workshop presenter, a community ECE mentor, and a college practical placement teacher. Simon regularly presents at various conferences, including the American Educational Research Association conference (2019) and Encounters with a Pedagogista: Co-labouring Pedagogy as an Ethical Relationship (2018). As a registered early childhood educator in Ontario, Simon has practised Indigenous pedagogy and curriculum at the Seneca College ECE Lab School for the past 15 years. For the last two years, Simon has been the Indigenous liaison between the lab school and First Peoples' Office at the college. Together with the Elder and Knowledge Holders, Simon has supported the lab school's staff as they begin to reflect on their role in answering the Truth and Reconciliation of Canada's Calls to Action for the ECEC field. Simon is currently an MA student in early childhood studies at Ryerson University. For her master's thesis, Simon has been investigating how Indigenous early childhood educators are making and holding space for Indigenous pedagogy in mainstream child care. Her research interests include Indigenous pedagogy and curriculum, decolonization, and land-based education.